Connecting the Dots

The Story of God's Work
Rescuing One Man's Heart and Life

Praise be to the God and Father of our Lord Jesus Christ, who has blessed us in the heavenly realms with every spiritual blessing in Christ.

For he chose us in him before the creation of the world to be holy and blameless in his sight. In love he predestined us for adoption to sonship through Jesus Christ, in accordance with his pleasure and will—

Ephesians 1:3-5

Blessed be the God and Father of our Lord Jesus Christ, the Father of mercies and God of all comfort, who comforts us in all our affliction, so that we may be able to comfort those who are in any affliction, with the comfort with which we ourselves are comforted by God.

2 Corinthians 1:3–4 *Oct 2023*

(English Standard Version)

Lisa,

Your baptism and testimony touched not only me, but many others around our family.

Like you, life has often been dark and traumatic but the hope reached out and delivered us from that prison! May this book encourage you and remind you it does not matter where we begin!

John

Connecting the Dots

The Story of God's Work Rescuing One Man's Heart and Life

Written by John M. Mayner

Copyright © 2022

Bible quotes in this book are from the
The Holy Bible, English Standard Version® (ESV®)
Copyright © 2001 by Crossway, a publishing ministry of
Good News Publishers. All rights reserved. ESV Text
Edition: 2016

This book is dedicated to several groups of people

First, to my wife, Melody, and our sons, Rob, and Andy, and my Aunt Sharon who walked with me through all of the difficult experiences. They have suffered much on my behalf as they watched me unsuccessfully carry many burdens alone until I sought help and worked through much of the trauma I have experienced.

Second, to those who have walked with me through the darker valleys of despair, encouraged me to keep going, and have been reminders of God's love, compassion, and grace in a broken world

Finally, to my friend, and brother,
James Lee Mayner,
who was not able to experience the joy
of being rescued when he took his own life
shortly before his 34th birthday.

June 25, 1957 – June 13, 1990

Special Thanks

I want to express my gratitude to several who have been extremely helpful in the writing of this book.

The first is Stephanie Anderson who spent a great deal of time reviewing and editing the rough draft. I have known Stephanie and her family for over twenty years and have been impressed by her integrity, character, faith, and genuine concern for others. She has walked through some very difficult times herself, experienced great loss, and battled cancer without losing her trust in God. Her story is one that should be shared as well because she is an amazing reflection of Christ.

The next is Mary Jane Wilt, someone you will come to know in the latter part of this book. She has been my counselor and has helped me process much of the traumatic experiences that have impacted my life. During the last several years I have spent hundreds of hours sharing about every aspect of my life and have cried so much in her office that I think her rug was ruined by all the salt water that ran off my cheeks as she just got a new one. Her commitment not only to this difficult process but to the Lord has allowed me to walk through the pain and see Christ in a different light. She has literally cried with me as I have shared the entirety of my experiences, helped me grasp the reality that the Lord has always been there – through everything - and find the elusive peace and joy I had never before been able to enjoy.

Much of my life's journey has been tumultuous to say the least. However, there have been quite a few people you will come to know in the following pages that have been powerful forces that have loved without judgment and who are extremely close friends.

Paul and Beryl Metko have mentored me since 1977 and showed great patience as I began to see faith as a daily experience. They have become family not only to me, but also to my wife and sons as well. Alan and Cindy MacLurg and Paul and Susan Winsinger have walked beside me since 1981 when we were students at Multnomah. They have remained faithful to the Lord and to my family and me through it all without expectation or recrimination. Eric and Christina Comparini are dear friends from Brazil who have been such an encouragement as we have watched their faith grow and remained connected despite all of the traveling both families have done. Matt Moffat is perhaps one of the most compassionate and gentle man I have ever known. We have shared many lunches, tears, and times of study together during the last eleven years as I have been processing all that has transpired. I often found myself crying in his office after some of the more difficult counseling sessions, but he has drawn closer to me as opposed to walking away.

Finally, I want to thank Jason Clarke, Nolan Tjaden, and Kristen Friend. They entered my life at a time when I had just about given up on the Lord being able to use me in any manner. Their transparency, grace, servant hearts, words of encouragement, and love have been a balm to my heart. Jason and Nolan's messages from the pulpit and personal interactions have not only reinforced things I believe but have also cut to the quick and convicted me to make changes in my heart and life because of their insight into the Scriptures. Jason was also the one who suggested that he could see me on the prayer team at the church. This opened an unexpected door that has allowed me to minister in a manner I never believed was even possible.

My love for each of you has only grown deeper as the days and years have gone by. May this book reflect the role you have played in my desire and ability to minister to others for the sake of the Kingdom.

Preface

> Trauma - **noun**
> trau·ma | \ ˈtrȯ-mə *also* ˈtrau̇- \
> Definition of *trauma*
> **1a:** an injury (such as a wound) to living tissue caused by an extrinsic agent
> **b:** a disordered psychic or behavioral state resulting from severe mental or emotional stress or physical injury
> **c:** an emotional upset
> **2:** an agent, force, or mechanism that causes trauma

Trauma has been a frequent companion throughout my life. Like so many others, my home of origin was a place of literal beatings, fear, degradation, and both sexual and verbal abuse, with little encouragement. However, teachers, unexpected friends, coworkers, counselors, neighbors, and foster parents became positive models for me to follow. As my high school graduation approached, I could not wait to move on to other things and put all of the painful experiences behind me. I was convinced that when I began a new life, in a new place, all of the trauma I experienced would fall by the wayside and become a long-forgotten part of my past.

However, I would discover that experiences in life seldom miraculously lose their pull and that they had a way of returning. I wrestled with how to navigate relationships within a seriously dysfunctional family. I was confused about what it meant to honor my parents when forgiving them was outweighed by the burdens of bitterness, anger, and even resentment. I had no idea as to how these things could be overcome and was troubled by my responses. I questioned whether God could ever love, accept, or even use me. During these times I was unable to see clearly enough to follow what Christ taught and modeled.

As the years went by, well-meaning people tried to encourage me, but my experiences were so foreign to them that they did not know what to do, so they pulled away. They sometimes asked if there was sin in my life and whether I had prayed about these things, or even availed myself of various religious experiences. At a critical juncture in my journey, despair took me to the point that living no longer seemed prudent or reasonable. Trying to escape the pain through an overdose led to a stay in the psychiatric ward at a hospital in Portland, Oregon.

Much of this happened while battling chronic nerve pain, over two dozen surgeries – scheduled and emergency – coupled with regularly recurring nightmares that resulted in days and weeks of despair. There have been times I have been angry at the Lord and asked difficult questions about the, "why's" and "what-ifs." From the depths of my being, I have cried out for relief from the pain and anguish that seemed to define my life. Sometimes, it was all I could do to get up each morning. I struggled to make sense of it all and my confidence that God was there would be seriously shaken.

In my brokenness I heard from God in a powerful way that led me to look at my life's journey from a very different perspective. It has allowed me to see how God, the creator of the universe, has orchestrated all of it. From the earliest of times to the present, the Lord has used specific individuals, experiences, the Bible, and His Holy Spirit to guide, mold, refine, convict, and direct me.

I must be honest; some of what follows will be difficult to read. Life is often messy, and people have free will to do good or evil. You will see how people and events shaped, and transformed, my heart and life. There is great pain and sorrow expressed in these pages, but they are countered by God's dramatic, loving, and compassionate work, joy, and discovery.

I have shared my journey both for those who are struggling with the messiness of life, living in the dark days of despair, or have given up hope, as well as for the family, friends, teachers, and counselors that have relationships with these individuals. This book does not offer specific answers, instead, it is meant to help shed light on the darkness and confusion resulting from serious trauma. Seldom is trauma something that can be instantly or instantaneously healed. Instead, there are victories, failures, and pain that must be faced if we are to find help and hope. My own journey has allowed me to come alongside others without judgment but with grace and compassion as they experience their own trials.

My hope is that *Connecting the Dots* brings encouragement and hope and reminds you that nothing in life is coincidental or accidental. While it will give you some insight into the life of someone who struggles with PTSD, anxiety, and depression, I pray that you might also be able to look into your own heart and life and see; again, or for the first time, that God is working in, and shaping, your own heart.

Chapter 1

Seeds in the Field

Like so many evenings, when living near Puget Sound, the fog covered everything with bone-chilling dampness. The moon was little more than a dim light in the sky, the stars almost nonexistent. It was an evening when families would normally be huddled inside, watching a favorite show, or doing homework, enjoying the warmth of a heater or fire. But that was not the case in the house where I grew up. Instead, my sister, one brother, and I were outside, on the lawn, watching my parents pushing, and screaming at, each other. We were crying, embarrassed in front of the neighbors' watching eyes, and terrified as we watched things predictably unfold. Our two youngest brothers remained in the house, but the door was open, and I could see them weeping, looking hurt, and confused. Like each of us, they were crying in their hearts for deliverance. Each of us wanted to be taken to a place of peace and rest. We wanted a "normal" family. We wanted God – or anyone – to rescue us. We were desperate, lost, and alone, trapped in the torrent of anger, accelerated by excessive alcohol, and acted out by two adults who lacked any sort of compass to point the way out of their selfishness or addictions.

As was often the case, neighbors had called the King County Sheriff's office to report another fight at the Mayners' home. But without the laws we have today, to protect children in extremely abusive situations, there was little the deputies could do unless my mother pressed charges, something she was never able to bring herself to do. Calls about our parents fighting, or concern about the disciplining of my siblings and me, meant we were not strangers to the deputies who normally came to the house in pairs. After they arrived, each of my parents was separated from the other one, had time to present their side of the story, and were then strongly encouraged to go back inside and stop the battle in the driveway. Even as a boy in elementary school, I knew something was amiss and that the daily experiences in my home of origin were anything but normal. As we went back inside, we all knew the drill. The neighbors would go back into their own homes, and close the drapes, as if nothing unusual happened. We would go to our rooms, shut the doors, and were expected to go right to sleep; something that seldom happened. While the deputies did what they could, the evening battles were not over. The scene in front of the house would take a turn for the worse as we were now on our dad's radar, and he was not able to channel his anger towards our mom. Since we were in our rooms and still crying from fear and confusion, he would storm down the stairs and enter our rooms to begin taking his anger out on us with belts, sticks, throwing us against the walls, and even holding us down and blowing smoke into our faces as he puffed his Marlboro's. Sometimes, when he did not want to go to each of our three rooms, he would scream for us to get upstairs. This was not a request. Instead, it was the announcement the night was not over. Once there, all five of us lined up against the wall where we would stand and either endure or have to watch as the others were violently abused. This was never a quiet, quick, event. Only when our dad wore himself out would we find solace in our rooms. Even then, our sleep was anything but peaceful. Most nights found me in my brother's bed as we held each other and sobbed.

In the early morning hours, we would rise to newscasts from KVI Seattle, the aroma of coffee percolating, and hopefully the smell of oatmeal as opposed to cold puffed wheat. Like the movie, *The Truman Show*, everything was then predictable, routine, and filled with a sullen stoicism. Our battles from the previous evening would play out again but with the added humiliation of going to school. There, we had to run another gauntlet with other kids whose parents mocked us, and made it clear we were the laughingstocks of the neighborhood. Early in our lives, my siblings and I learned that other kids usually reflected the attitudes picked up in their own homes.

We were on a treadmill and could not get off. We lived in a world of terror that showed no mercy whether we were at home, school, or even sleeping. Like inmates, in a prison ruled by thugs, we endured, ye without hope. Fear reigned supreme and each of us attempted to navigate life in our own way. Despite our best efforts, the battle to find rest for our hearts and souls would fail. These failures led each of us down dark paths not only while in our home of origin, but also later in life.

Sometimes I share about my childhood experiences and people are surprised, as they see me today and think I have it together. However, hidden by a façade of normalcy, the real me remains – hidden, shattered, weary from experiencing so much pain. My pillow is regularly damp from the tears that flow freely at night, as I relive the terrors in my nightmares. These assaults and accusations are constant. They leave me drained, lifeless, and, often, without hope. Unlike a broken leg, or other visible medical issue, my siblings and I suffer in silence and shame trying to make sense of it all. Some of you might be reading this and have no idea what this kind of life would be like. Others, who live their lives in the same shadows, are reminded of their own painful journeys. Most of us will have moments in our lives where we ask difficult questions about God and life itself. Our travels through these traumatic experiences force us to look at who we really are and face our brokenness because some truths are only discovered when we are totally broken. Often, this happens at the point where we have lost all hope – perhaps even considering ending our lives. As I look back, it is clear that my journey of faith began in the very home where I experienced so much pain.

In my feeble efforts to stay out of the fray with others in the neighborhood on the way to and from school, my older brother Jim, and I would leave as early as possible. Often, we went through what we called, *the swamp*, a dark, soggy, wooded, area between the road and our elementary school. Normally, we stopped at one particular log where we sat and talked about anything to take our minds off of the previous evening's experiences. It was where we laughed together and knew we were untouchable. It was a place of solace. Since Jim and I shared a downstairs room, he tried to look out for me as much as he could. I was the sensitive one who lacked courage while he was more physical and assertive. I poured myself into school while he focused on the two *F's*, football and fighting. At the time, both of us found marginal success in these avenues of escape. We were sometimes late to school because of talking too long, but we normally ensured we made it to school on time as that was one less reason for our dad to pounce. This was easily done by listening to the school buses traverse the road just behind our little area of peace. In fact, I really enjoyed getting to school in time to watch the janitor hoist the flag. But that was not the main reason I wanted to arrive early and avoid prying eyes.

We attended Camelot Elementary, in the Federal Way School District. All students became familiar with the lore associated with the story of *Camelot*. In fact, there was an actual *sword-in-the-stone* displayed prominently outside of the main entrance. Each year there was a school wide tournament and all of us were given the opportunity to pull the sword from the stone. For Jim and me, this was our ticket out of our dystopian home life. On countless mornings, we visited that *'stone'* and tried every way we could to pull the sword out. Each time, it was the same result, failure. It seemed as if escape was always just beyond reach. Often, after these failed attempts, Jim and I would sit with our backs against the wall adjacent to the stone numb with the realization that there might not be any escape from our plight. I entered school in tears hundreds of times during my six years there. Since I could not find success and escape through these means, I sought to earn praise from my teachers. However, other students also had some say in how I fared. The weakest link is often the victim of bullies, and it was clear who that weak link was - me.

Recesses were a time of humiliation and depravation as others prevented me from playing four square and other games or using any of the various play structures. They became experts who knew just how to push me beyond the point where I could control my emotions. This in turn resulted in additional laughter and mocking. By second grade I had developed a serious stuttering problem that further alienated me from most of my classmates. However, there were some who were kind to me. They seemed to understand I was drowning in a storm that engulfed me each day. Although I struggled at recess, Jim made it clear he would level anyone who messed with him. Unfortunately, he was two years older and had a different recess than mine. Our only touch points were before and after school. The same was true of my older sister, Shelley, and my two younger brothers, Tony, and Mike. In many ways, my world narrowed to just Jim and me. Shelley was her own person as she is four years older and had her own room since she was the only girl in the family. Tony, eleven months younger than me, and Mike, four years, younger than me, shared the other room downstairs. While all of us played together, the bonds between them and me were not as strong as the one I had with Jim. It would be decades before Shelley, Mike, and I would have significant connections. However, my relationship with Tony never grew into anything beyond being of the same blood.

Throughout first through sixth grades at Camelot, there were two things that helped me move forward: books and an adult who was safe and listened.

I loved the school library because silence was strictly enforced. It was a place where bullies were quieted, exploration encouraged, and the hustle and bustle, associated with moving hundreds of kids through a school day, disappeared. While there, time seemed to move slower. I did not have to perform or compete. It became my own little sanctuary. I found that books could take me to distant lands, enlarge my world, and enchant my soul. They gave me a level of escape not found elsewhere in my life. I became a voracious reader of almost anything I could get my hands on. This era was a time of great innovation and exploration, so I read about the space program and early open-heart surgeries.

Another place I found rest and peace during the school day, was with my speech therapist, Mrs. Williams. She worked with me for 15 minutes, two or three times each week, between third and sixth grade. Her role was to help me address the stuttering problem, but she also became the one adult who consistently seemed to enjoy my company. I still remember her smile, how she always placed her hand over mine, and how happy she was both with my progress and just seeing me. At the time, she seemed old, but looking back, she was probably in her mid-thirties. Our time together became moments of tranquility for me. It was where I shared my heart. She communicated her concern for me and allowed me to share what was happening in my life. I felt safe. Our time also brought out something that was seldom seen during those years, a smile.

After moving on to Kilo Junior High, Jim and I continued to visit our special log on the way to school but we had to be aware of time as Kilo was a mile or so beyond Camelot. As Jim and I began making different friends, our times of walking together became fewer. I often made the trek alone but always stopped at the log and took a break.

During junior high, my bullies intensified their well-practiced attacks, aided by my very delayed entrance into puberty. These boys were relentless and took every opportunity to let me know where I stood. Just as they sought to establish their place in life, I also wanted a place – anywhere but there so I began reading about UFO's. I was convinced of their existence and activity. I also believed that if I could contact them, they would literally whisk me away from all my worsening problems at home and school. The log was where I looked heavenward, cupped my hands around my mouth, and called out for rescue. Yes, I actually did this hundreds of times and these were not casual cries into the dark early morning skies. They were groans from deep within my being, desperate pleas for help as I was sinking into the mire of anger, bitterness, rage, hopelessness, as a darkness began to descend upon my heart. These things transfixed my entire being to the point that I seriously began to contemplate how I could end my life.

And yet, there were moments of light along the way. Throughout my years in elementary and junior high, there were some neighbors that reached out to the Mayner kids. One family lived next door and were strong Catholics who tried to honestly live their faith. While they cared for us kids, they did not have any patience with my parents. I recall there seemed to be some level of tension between them and my mom and dad. I never dwelled on, or figured out, if there was jealousy on the part of my parents as we enjoyed our time with the neighbors or if it related more to lifestyle. This family took us to school plays and sometimes even gave us a ride home from school when the rain really poured – something that happened often in the Pacific Northwest. They also ensured we went to catechism classes one night a week at St Vincent DePaul Parish. Eventually Jim and I completed the requisite classes to receive our first communions. Their faith was not something totally foreign to me as my mom's parents, who lived in Portland, were faithful Catholic's. Like our neighbors, they too took us to mass.

Frequently, we traveled south to spend time with my maternal grandparents and Aunt Sharon in Portland. Although our relationship with my dad's parents was less than enjoyable, all of us loved Grandma and Grandpa Foreman. They lived in a small, post-war, home located in the southeast part of town. With five children, these trips were cramped, with four of us in the back seat of the station wagon and my youngest brother seated in the front, between mom and dad. My memories of those trips are filled with mixed emotions. Although my grandparents' home was another place where we felt safe, and could relax, the actual journey between Federal Way and Portland was anything but restful. Our car seemed to continually break down and the air was heavy with smoke from my dad's cigarettes because he insisted on smoking throughout the trip – with the windows closed. This meant we were not only in close proximity to one another, but also, endured itchy eyes and dry throats along with the regular tensions, arguments, and slaps to the face as we traveled. These journeys often began on Friday evenings, when my dad arrived home from working at Boeing, and ended late Sunday night.

Somehow, during our time at my grandparents, things seemed calmer, more respectful, and fun. We were allowed to play without being hit or yelled at, as my dad knew he should not go after us kids the way he did at home. During Saturday evenings we watched *Portland Wrestling* with my grandmother, as my parents were usually given money and told to go out. When they left, all of us breathed a sigh of relief and knew we could totally relax as we watched Jimmy Snuka and Dutch Savage jump around the ring wrestling *The Nature Boy*, Rick Flair, or the *Royal Kangaroos*. We always laughed when the bad guys did some dastardly deed and my grandmother threw her slipper at the television and asked, "Did you see that?" At the time, my aunt Sharon either lived in the house or was in nursing school at Emmanuel Hospital School of Nursing. Like my grandparents, she would play a crucial role in our lives – especially mine. Sunday mornings were special because they attended mass at the *Ascension Catholic Church*. I enjoyed the more ornate statues than those at St. Vincent De Paul Parish, as well as the most exquisite paintings on the ceiling in Monastery just down the street. My sense of being in the presence of God was strong and I never tired of the liturgy as it had a special pull on me. It was there, in those beautiful settings, that I decided I wanted to be a priest. At the time, I had no idea what that meant but my mind was settled on it.

Unlike the protestant churches I have attended throughout the last four decades, the Catholic churches were places of quiet solitude. I enjoyed the structure, formality, and appreciated the times when we kneeled to pray. These churches left me in awe as I considered the beautiful statues and art throughout their buildings. The solemnity of the entire service spoke to me. It was in these houses of worship that I began to consider the possibility that there was a God. At the time, I had little understanding of why that man, Jesus, hung on a cross. However, I sensed this was important, meaningful.

During this same period, another family began to play a part in my life. This family lived further up the street, and like our immediate neighbors, they too were people of faith.

While we were not the best of children, they often opened their home up for the Mayner boys to come have a snack after school. More importantly, they let us come and listen as the father used his HAM radio to talk with people in Central and South America. Sometimes, he would even let us talk to them. Years later I discovered these voices were Protestant missionaries the parents had worked with. What could be better than homemade cookies and talking with people who were living in exotic lands and doing cool things? These times became special moments as I knew they did not let just anyone enjoy this experience with them. For once in my life, I felt extra special. But their care did not stop there. During the summer, they invited us to something called *5 Day Clubs*. There, Jesus was presented a little differently than in the quietness of what I enjoyed in the Catholic church. In fact, each day they asked about receiving Jesus into your heart. I quickly discovered that if you received Jesus (whatever that meant!), you also collected extra cookies. Once I realized this, I received Jesus quite often during several summers. Somehow, I seemed to have missed the main point, but the adults were patient and understanding.

It was apparent to me that those who followed this Jesus – my grandparents and neighbors - were quite different from others. It was clear that the lives of my grandparents and these neighbors were quite different from my own parents. Their examples planted a seed that would continue to grow in the coming decades as I navigated the pain, sorrows, and joys in life.

Chapter 2
Friends and Foes

Junior high meant I had to learn how to navigate school, life, and bullies, on my own and without Jim's interventions. But because Kilo drew students from several elementary schools, I had a clean slate with a large number of students. While there are many kids who had thrived on putting others down, and humiliating them, there were many of us who had lived on the fringes, waiting for any opportunity to connect with others. But would I find these connections? Although I had played some baseball, my body was extremely weak and out of shape, so it was clear that sports were not the answer. However, opportunities presented themselves, some at school, and others involved playing an instrument and joining the Civil Air Patrol.

Just like at Camelot, I was searching not only for connections, but also a place where I could be someone worthwhile and worthy of praise. One day I heard Mr. Hansen, the basketball coach, talk about needing someone to push the broom and clean up the court before games and during half-time. Since I liked him, I volunteered. It was fairly straight forward but there was an entirely new element involved, an energetic audience. At our first home game, I stood by the sidelines, alone in the shadows, waiting to do my job. Despite being similar to a water boy for the football team, I wanted *coach* to be proud of my work. At the end of the second quarter, when the buzzer sounded, the teams left the court and headed to the locker rooms. This was my go time. Like a player before an important game, I had butterflies in the pit of my stomach. For a moment, I froze, wondering what I was thinking when I volunteered for this very public role. However, I had made the commitment, and I was going to fulfill it. Despite my goose bumps, I began to push the broom across the shiny, smooth, court. I had nothing but fear driving me. I feared disappointing Coach Hansen. I dreaded what other students were going to say. I never considered the possibility that the next few minutes might change not only my time at school, but my life as well.

Even as a boy, I ran hot and sweated easily, and this task was taking more physical, and emotional, energy than I thought it would. Soon, large, dark, circles of perspiration formed under my arm pits, and I knew my body odor would assault anyone who ventured close to me. My heart sank. I wanted to drop the broom, quit, run home, and bury my head. However, I was unable to do anything but face forward, going through the motions, while inside I was breaking into ever smaller pieces. Once again, I was going to be embarrassed, only this time, it would not be before a small group of bullies. Instead, it would happen with a larger crowd. It was as if I invited an entire elementary school to come and watch me fail again. I was beginning to panic, and tears welled up in my already reddened eyes. However, before the salty liquid flowed freely down my cheeks, a sudden rumbling began in the crowd. At first, it was a low vibration, barely recognizable, but quickly it became a chant from everyone. They were shouting, "Go Johnny go." I was puzzled as no one ever called me Johnny. Now I knew it, I would be humiliated, and everyone would know who I was. To this day I cannot explain what happened next, or why I did it, but I began to dance with that broom as I went across the floor. Suddenly, the roar grew even louder, and now, even the cheer leaders were involved. Oh, this was the sweet ticket I needed. My heart leaped as the sound resonated in my ears and throughout the gym. I did not want the moment to end. Were they making fun of me? Who cared? They were having fun, and I was enjoying it too. Finally, I was somebody! The motivation of the crowd no longer mattered. For the first time ever, I existed. I was known. Somehow, it freed something in me that began to break the protective shell which had encased me during my early life. What completed the night was the coach telling me I did a great job. I still remember walking home that night. It was dark and there was a drizzle of rain, but I floated above it all. I continued doing this for each home game and both adults and students actually patted me on the back. They encouraged me to continue my *performance's* as it made half time more enjoyable. The next day, there were some noticeable changes when I went into my classes. Other students actually spoke to me, and we laughed about my impromptu dance routine. This helped me discover a group of friends who seemed to like, and accept, me. It was the first time I ever used humor to break the ice. It was clear that people wanted to laugh and, if you helped them do that, they would allow you into their groups. This is something that has helped me connect with people for over fifty years.

This new connection with other students helped make my time at Kilo much easier. Further, since we were not stuck in the same classroom all day, there were only a couple bullies in my class at any one time – something I was now able to deal with, especially since I had friends who backed me up. While at school, I found several teachers who seemed to understand that I was trying to figure life out. Of course, every student was, but they seemed to take a special interest in helping me explore and understand the world around me and grow academically. Two teachers still stand out in my mind, Miss Morin, and Mrs. Maze.

Miss Morin was my typing teacher. A single woman and veteran teacher, her face was both wrinkled and scarred from acne, but her eyes were soft, vibrant, and communicated genuine concern. While many thought she had a chip on her shoulder, I was somehow able to connect with her in a way that helped me focus while in her class. My fingers flew as I became more proficient and the grades on my assignments encouraged me further. By the end of seventh grade, I was also one of five students she let use the new *IBM Selectric Typewriter*. The idea that there were different balls, with different fonts, and your fingers would no longer get stuck between keys, made typing even more enjoyable. At the time, I had no idea how important typing would be for me in the future.

Unlike grade school, when teachers put gold stars on your assignments, Miss Morin put a smiley face and actual comments. She also made time to ask about my day and reinforced her words of encouragement on my papers. Seldom did I leave that room without feeling better not just about myself, but also life in general. This was another life lesson I would carry with me in; we are all in need of words that will motivate and help us make it through another day.

Having my typing class right before lunch allowed me to endure some of the rudeness that came from several vocal bullies in the cafeteria. Once I was sitting with my friends, I was able to ignore shouted comments and face the rest of the day.

My final class of the day was English, taught by Mrs. Maze. She was a much younger woman than Miss Morin and was soft spoken, with a pleasant demeanor that reminded me of my Aunt Sharon and Grandma Foreman. She seemed to know what each student needed and, somehow, even the air seemed different in her classroom. Her class allowed me to end each school day on a positive note. Mrs. Maze talked about sentence structure and had copious writing assignments, but my favorite part was the assigned books. One particular book caught my attention, *Run Baby Run*, by Nicki Cruz. It was the story of a young man in the Bronx who was caught up in the gang culture but eventually responded to a preacher and decided to turn his life around. It was the first time I saw someone else express some of my own thoughts and feelings. While I did not know exactly where the Bronx was on a map, I understood a great deal about this young man. Like him, I was searching and striking out at others. His life was changed, just as mine would be, because someone demonstrated love when we knew we were broken. It remains one of my all-time favorite books. As I reflect on the various assignments, and books she had us read, I am still amazed that she was able to do this in a public school. It was years later that I discovered she was a Messianic Jew who saw her role in the classroom as a calling from God.

While these two teachers really cared about me, there was another adult in my life, who unlike Miss Morin and Mrs. Maze, did not have my best interests at heart. The connection to him began when Jim and I joined Civil Air Patrol.

I could never understand why we were not allowed to join the Cub, or Boy, Scouts as their programs seemed like great opportunities for boys to mature, have fun, and be out of the house. Of course, at that age, I was attracted to the uniforms and fun part of their programs as opposed to the character-building aspects. One family, the Brown's, lived in a nearby cul-de-sac, and had two sons and a daughter we knew from school. Although the boys were two and three years older than either Jim or me, we discovered they were involved with Civil Air Patrol. They attended weekly meetings, wore Air Force uniforms, and seemed like heroes to me. Since my dad worked at Boeing supporting the various Mercury and Apollo Space programs, and I loved watching the flag go up each morning while in elementary school, this seemed like it might be the bill to help both of us fit in better. After some talks between both sets of parents, we were allowed to join.

In short order, we became members of the Green River Composite Squadron that focused on Land Search and Rescue (LSAR) and communications. Civil Air Patrol is an Auxiliary of the Air Force, and the individual squadrons are supervised by adult volunteers known as *Senior Cadets*. Some of these volunteers were in the Air Force, or a reserve component; were civilian pilots; or just enjoyed helping young men and women. While both Jim and I needed positive discipline in our lives, we also wanted adventure. We decided to train for the LSAR element as it seemed like a lot more fun than learning Morse Code. We trained in first aid, land navigation, and ground search techniques. Both of us enjoyed them, but never progressed too fast in rank as we really did not know how to study all the required material on our own. We also had no idea how much money it cost to participate in this program. Neither of my parents were totally committed to this venture, and it was only later that I discovered the Brown's covered these costs for us. Although Jim was a normal size for his age, I remained short and super skinny, and had small feet. This meant that my uniforms hung poorly on my frame and had to an extra pair of winter socks so the boots would not give me blisters. None of this mattered because the weekly meetings were a time of relative freedom. I enjoyed learning about the Air Force, loved drilling, heard from actual pilots, and went on my first ride in an airplane.

It was during these meetings that Jim and I discovered one particular Senior Cadet who seemed to take an interest in us. This man was "the Major." However, he had ulterior motives. At first, we thought he was the most amazing man as he took us for rides in a small plane, had a cool red Ford *Mustang*, showed us all sorts of weapons, and cast a spell on us as he talked about his work with both the Air Commandoes and Defense Intelligence Agency in Vietnam. It did not matter that neither Jim or I understood anything about alphabet agencies, or that people who are associated with them seldom speak openly about their activities. What mattered was that a "real American hero" was spending time with us. His stories left me spellbound and piqued my interest not only to read about what was happening in Vietnam, but also anything military. Meanwhile, the Major was also learning about my brother and me so that he could continue grooming us.

Sometime during my second year of participating in Civil Air Patrol, he took Jim and me up to a training area we all knew as *Ranger Creek*. It was familiar to us as we had flown there and spent a few weekends practicing map reading and going through compass exercises that tested our ability to move across wooded, mountainous, terrain. Although snow was on the ground, I do not remember encountering any problems on the roads and even if we did, I was not worried as the man we were with was an Air Commando and could handle anything. We sat in the vehicle as he gave us coffee and said it had bourbon in it as it would help warm our insides and, "… make men out us." Jim and I took to that like a kitten to milk and it became our routine whenever he came to pick us up for these trips. Somehow, we loved sharing that beverage as it made us feel connected and it was "our little secret." As things developed, he would let one of us spend the night with him in his apartment and promised the other one a different time. I still remember the excitement as I looked forward to when it would be my turn. When the time finally came, I was overjoyed.

He fixed a simple dinner and his apartment seemed very dark, not just in lighting, but for some reason, I recall it feeling a little creepy. The Major showed me to the spare bedroom where I would sleep, and I went to bed. However, there would be no rest on this night. At some point he silently slipped into the room and then crawled into bed and lay next to me. I was not only very naïve about sexual matters, but I was also confused as to why he has there next to me. Shortly after this, my confusion became real, raw, deep terror. My heart raced and I began to panic in a way that went beyond that which I experienced when my dad was on his drunken tirades. What happened over the next few hours destroyed me on so many levels. While I begged for him to stop, he laughed and continued these brutal acts. My trust of adult males went from minimal to nonexistent. I wanted to run but was trapped. I wanted to fight back but was too weak. I would have done anything to be anywhere but there. At some point, I just shut down. I thought of being at the log with Jim. It was as though I could not comprehend, accept, or understand what was happening. Eventually, he left the room but despite my exhaustion, fear kept me awake. I was shaking and sobbed from the reality not just of what had occurred but also for being totally powerless. I spent the remainder of the night sitting with my back to the wall, arms around my knees, weeping in the corner furthest from the door. My mind was overwhelmed, and I could hardly move or think beyond basic questions. Why did he do this? What had I done to deserve this lot in life? Where was God? The only thing I knew was that this man did something terrible to me and I had absolutely no power over the situation.

In the morning the Major came to my room and told me it was time to go home. The caring attitude of all previous conversations was no longer there. His face was devoid of emotion. There was no sense that he was sorry about anything that happened; it was as if nothing unusual took place during the previous evening. After this, he fixed himself breakfast and told me I had not earned mine, so he sat down and ate in front of me as I stood with my back against the wall and watched him. The ride back to my house was absolutely silent. What could I say? I was in shock and leaned as close to the passenger door as I could while holding back the torrent of tears. They would eventually come when I ran to my room and closed the bedroom door. I still remember considering the option of opening the car door and jumping out on the road with hopes that a car would run me over. Any hope of happiness evaporated. I was humiliated on levels I had never experienced. As a silent rage rose inside my heart, I felt more alone than ever before. My mind contemplated who I might tell but I kept coming up with one answer; it was my fault so it would be better not to say anything.

There was so much shame and pain involved with this experience that I did not speak about it to anyone for years. However, in 1986, while my wife and I were living in Escondido, California Jim came for a brief visit. We talked and laughed for hours until there was a pause and Jim shared his own story of being violated by the Major. That night, Jim and I did what we had done so many times as children; we held each other and sobbed. For the first time in my life, I spoke about the absolute worst night of my life. The wounds were once again open, and raw. The pain was as fresh as the experience itself and once again, the nightmares were more intense. We were adrift in the storm, clinging to each other in desperation, hoping to be rescued. I would remain adrift in this ocean of pain for another 17 years before speaking of that event to anyone else. Most of the latter part of my experience would occur without my brother by my side.

Chapter 3
Are You My Mother (or Father)?

Those moments with Jim in Escondido not only took me back to the events of the evening but also reminded me of the seeming lack of concern by either of our parents. While they had never been heavily involved with our lives, it always struck me as a bit odd that they did not seem concerned about the Major's attention to us or all the time we had spent with him. If that went unnoticed, they should have noted the sudden change that followed when neither Jim or I spent any more time with the Major, quit Civil Air Patrol, never talked about him, and he stopped coming by the house. I was left with the question, "Who are my parents?"

In his classic children's book, *Are You My Mother?*, P.D. Eastman tells the story of a young bird who searches for his mother because she was not there when he hatched from the egg. We then follow the various interactions this young bird has on this quest. The book's question has puzzled me throughout most of my life. Much of what I knew was anecdotal at best, but some critical pieces were missing not just in my own memories of when I was a child, but also as an adult. When we discovered aspects of their lives, it was usually through conversations with my aunt, Grandma and

Grandpa Foreman or a newly discovered cousin of my dad's. It was as though our parents were covert agents who needed to keep their true identities secret because neither of them shared with us even when we asked direct questions as adults. Often, I wondered if they really were not my parents and hoped that one day I would find my real family. What I did not realize is a possible scenario would present itself when I was in my early thirties.

In 1990, I was stationed at Travis AFB in California, doing my job as an In-Service Recruiter. I was responsible for helping Airmen separating from Active Duty find a place in an Air Force Reserve unit near their home. During an interview with a young airman who had completed his time on active duty, I wrote down his address, where he was born, and his birthdate. When he told me his birthdate was August 29, 1959, I stopped and chuckled a little. I then asked for the place he was born, and he said, "Seattle." I was born in Seattle on that date as well. I asked about the hospital where he was born and he replied, "Burien General." Really? He continued, stating that he was delivered by Dr. Underwood, the very same doctor identified on my birth certificate. When I heard this, I sat back in my chair speechless. I was considering the odds of all these things actually happening, and the possibilities this opened. I sarcastically asked, "What are my real parents like?" For a moment, he too was surprised, and then we had a good laugh. Although he came to our house for dinner a couple times after that, I lost touch with him, but the question stayed with me for years. As much as I wanted it to be true, I have too much of my Grandpa Foreman's characteristics to not be associated with the correct family of origin. I was left with my original question about my parents.

My father, Richard (Dick) Lee, was born in Portland on January 20, 1930, to Frank and Anna Mayner. His dad was a construction laborer, and his mom found work at Libby's canning. The fact that Anna often spoke about Grandpa Mayner being, "just a laborer," told me a great deal about how she felt about her husband. She was embarrassed that he had not gone off to war but – instead - remained in the states to work on construction projects. I know little of his story but hers is perhaps the most interesting as her parents initially moved from Germany to Odessa Russia, on the Black Sea, because they did not like the Kaiser. However, they found even more disappointment with the Russians, so they immigrated to the United States in 1900. After arriving, they lived on a German settlement in Pierre, South Dakota before finally heading west to Portland, Oregon. Grandma Mayner would often tell my wife and I that, "We were from Russia but ate with forks." This sense of superiority permeated much of her demeanor and not only impacted my father, but also each of us children during our occasional visits to their home. Grandpa always seemed subservient to her but had a ready smile and Chicklets for each of us kids – something that is still a pleasant memory of mine. Later we discovered he used to play the steel guitar but had obviously given it up as we never saw, or heard, him play. Had the relationship between my parents and him been better, I think all of us would have enjoyed his company.

My dad was an only child who lived a rigid, structured, life that included attending church with his mother. From an early age two unmistakable messages were clear; first there was little time for fun. Second, one needed to accept Christ as Savior and focus on His imminent return

During his school years, dad had a knack for math, loved to read, put model airplanes together, and enjoyed electric trains. Prior to my grandmother's death in 2003, I only knew about an Uncle Ray who I met only a couple of times while growing up. As far as any of us knew, that was his only living relative because he never mentioned anyone else. After Grandma passed away, I was able to track down Serge, one of my dad's cousins who lived in Texas. During a phone conversation and lengthy correspondence, he recalled only two times their paths crossed, despite Serge's parents living in Portland. With a sadness in his voice, Serge said that both encounters occurred when my dad was in his teen years. During those brief visits, my father became upset when Serge tried to play with the train and help with a model airplane. My dad aggressively made it clear he was never to touch his things again.

After graduating from high school, my dad joined the Oregon Air National Guard and trained to work on radars. He was mustered to active duty with an Aircraft Warning and Control Squadron 164 miles west of Nome, Alaska in the middle of the Bering Sea, on Saint Lawrence Island. He was part of Detachment A-4 stationed at Gambell between May 1951 and August 1952. It was referred to as, "The Rock," because of the permafrost and barren landscape. The island is home to the Yup'ik Eskimos and even today only has 1,400 people on the island, but more than 2.7 million seabirds return to nest each year. It was a remote, windswept, desolate, outpost. A few amenities and supplies arrived by air, when possible, but often came by dogsled teams. Although we never saw photos, or heard many stories of his experiences there, he did talk about trading a broken shotgun for a stuffed seal pup which we saw whenever we visited dad's parents. However, I was never allowed to touch it until I returned from being stationed overseas. After returning to Oregon, my dad was hired by the Boeing Company in Seattle and worked there from 1955 through 1989, when he retired. Like his role on St Lawrence, much of his career was spent working on classified projects. The two that we knew the most about related to support for the various Apollo launches from Cape Canaveral, Florida, and the E-3 AWACS surveillance aircraft which the Air Force still uses to control the airspace where our forces operate.

Although our evenings almost always suffered from his drunkenness, he also built televisions, made model airplanes, and was a keen strategist. Many evenings found him at the kitchen table, looking over his glasses as he glued, sanded, and painted lifelike model airplanes. He then hung these in our rooms downstairs where I often dreamed of what it would be like to fly in one. While we enjoyed seeing the newest model, and marveled at his exacting detail work, we were never allowed to do more than sit, watch, and bring him beers. All of us knew not to disturb him while he was busy with his little projects. His love of aircraft grew over the years as he began building and flying radio-controlled planes. And, just like the building of models, we were only servants and observers.

Another area where his artistic talents were shone was with his model railroads. He loved the whole process, forming the mountains, cutting the track, painting the landscape, and building the little towns. More than once I earned a serious smacking with whatever was available when he discovered I had played with one of his trains. He made it clear his toys belonged to him alone. But, for a few moments of joy, all of us took those opportunities despite the price we would pay later.

Dad also loved working on anything electronic, and during the 60's *Heathkit* put out all sorts of electronics that individuals could build – much like people do with computers today. He built several televisions and a stereo that lasted most of our growing up years. Like his models, he seldom counted the hours it took to do these projects. Instead, he measured most things by how many beers it took.

When not doing these things, e enjoyed playing board games, but these were not the children's variety one often plays with kids. Instead, they were *Avalon Hill* strategy games or chess which forced you to make decisions about the best use of your specific units. I enjoyed the strategy and wanted to learn more about how units should be employed. However, I also understood that I had better be ready to explain a poor move, or I would be disciplined severely. Despite this, I still sought a connection with him and played whenever he asked me to join him. As I entered my teenage years, I began to beat him until one day he yanked *Blitzkrieg* off the table, threw it on the floor, and began hitting and berating me for winning. That was the last game I ever played with him. What could have been a great opportunity for finding some common ground became another painful memory. He never understood that much of my love for thinking strategically came from the games we played, and it is something that served me well throughout my military career. I often wonder how different our lives might have been had he shared his knowledge on so many subjects and enjoyed watching us progress. It not only could have been something to make us closer, but it would have bolstered our confidence levels. While my dad's reactions always baffled me, my mother puzzled me even more.

Like him, she too was born in Portland to her parents, Clair and Lois Foreman on January 29, 1936. At the time, my grandfather worked for the US Forest Service as a Civilian Conservation Corps Advisor, a Ranger, a forest firefighter, and mechanic. Since the roads were not what we have today, they lived in many of the towns near Mt Hood, including Zig Zag and Government Camp. While it sounds idyllic in many ways, he was often gone so my grandmother was responsible for raising Betty alone, in a rugged environment. The one story we know from this time related to *Buster* the bobcat. Apparently, he was found as a young cub and my mother was able to keep him for a pet. He was keen on keeping Betty in check but was also a loyal companion while they lived up near Mt Hood. Like many fathers during WWII, her dad was drafted into the Navy in 1944 and was in the south Pacific until 1947. During these years, my grandmother worked outside the home, and they lived with my mom's maternal grandparents and aunt. While there, my mother became very fond of Grandma and Grandpa O'Brien. My mom's sister, Sharon, was born in November 1947. This was not appreciated by my mother and remained a bone of contention throughout her life. For eleven years she had been the focus of everyone's attention, but once my grandfather returned from the war, and my aunt was born, she ceased being the center of the universe.

Mom attended Ascension Catholic Grade School and then public schools for both middle and high school. Although she graduated from Washington High School in 1954, she never took to her studies and had little interest in either attending college or going to work. Instead, she wanted to leave her parents' home as soon as possible and be a mother. At some point, she met up with my dad and was immediately smitten. Their relationship seemed to move quickly from hanging out to wanting to get married. Since the Obrien's had moved to Seattle, she went to live with them when my dad was hired by Boeing. Shortly after this, my parents were married in March 1955 and moved into a small tract home overlooking SEA-TAC airport. Over the next four years they had four children, but this did not mean the marriage was going well. It seemed as though my mom thought kids would automatically be connected and loyal to their mother, but she was overwhelmed with all the responsibility associated with having four young children in such a short time span. So, during the summer of 1960, my aunt came to help with us kids and, apparently, I seldom left her side. Recently, when Sharon told me about that summer, it made sense why I have always been so bonded with her as opposed to my biological mother.

In 1963, when my parents discovered they were having my youngest brother, the decision was made to move to a new location in Federal Way, just south of Seattle. At the time, it was a small town that was just being developed but is now an incorporated city. Boeing was expanding so fast that houses were needed to handle the new influx of people and sprawling communities grew all around the Puget Sound Region.

While dad worked long hours, mom tried her hand at working at fast food locations, a pizza joint, and Skippers Fish and Chips. Nothing seemed to last too long for her as temper did not mix with being in customer service. She also tried being a homemaker but was never able to connect with any of her children in her role as a mother.

Although she ensured all of our lunches were ready before we left for school, much of her time revolved around soap operas, baking, and visiting with friends she made while living in the previous house. I do not recall being comforted by her or being tucked into bed at any time during my childhood. However, her voice was often heard throughout the neighborhood as she cupped her hands around her mouth and yelled, "Shell, Jim, John, Tone [this is not a typo, she referred to Tony as 'Tone.'], Mike," numerous times. This call was often imitated by other kids in the neighborhood and, while it bothered us on one level, it eventually became funny to me as no other parent did this. These requests did not demand immediate attention until the fourth or fifth time when her voice became a desperate shrill. We knew we would get smacked around for not coming right away but those extra moments of peace and freedom were precious. While mom wanted to have dinner as a family, we seldom ate together and when we did, there were constant arguments, slaps to the face, water tossed at you for the smallest accident, and plates thrown around the kitchen.

For whatever reason, my mother struggled with her self-esteem and verbally attacked anyone she felt threated by – both in the family and outside it. Her tirades only added to the issues we had in the neighborhood and left us totally embarrassed throughout all my years living in that house. Even when we made inroads with other kids in the neighborhood, we knew jokes about her. To her credit, she let us go to various church and school functions with some neighbors I mentioned in chapter one, but I cannot recall either of my parents attending any activity. I want to believe she was acting out of concern for our well-being, but always sensed she just wanted us out of the house. My mother seemed scared to go very many places, and I always attributed it to her being so large but could never totally figure out what prevented her from being comfortable around others. Yet she had a flair for the dramatic and seemed to know what to say, or how to act, to achieve a desired outcome.

During one of our trips down to Portland, the brakes went out and our car hit another one. Dad somehow managed to get the car completely stopped using the parking brake, curb, and, of course, the other vehicle. When the other driver exited his car, he made a beeline for ours. He was an older man, obviously used to physical labor and his beet red face was contorted in anger. He began screaming at my father, which only exasperated my dad. However, mom quickly exited the car and held her neck, talking about the pain she was experiencing. When she got the man's attention, she pointed to the car, and while I did not know what she said, I believe holding her neck and pointing to us kids did the trick. The man returned to his car and drove off. When my parents returned to our vehicle, one of us asked about mom's neck and were told to shut up. It might have been a miraculous healing, but I believe she knew her actions would help move the man along. She never mentioned this again or had any problems with her neck or back throughout the rest of her life. That was when I realized that she would manipulate people to do what she wanted. This ability would eventually drive innumerable wedges between individuals in our family. Once the cause of these divisions was identified, she would strike out at each of her living children and seek to destroy each opportunity for us to come together.

Her life as a child, and dreams of what being a mother would be like, were a far cry from the reality she lived in our home. It was anything but pleasant and happy. Like us, she too was physically abused by my dad which caused her to retreat further into her imaginary world because the real one was too painful. During one of these arguments, my dad actually fired his .22 into the mattress. He claimed it was an accident, but I always felt he did this to intimidate her and make it clear she should not question him. Sometimes her cries mixed with our own and, once again, the darkness descended on our house and hearts.

Mom often tried to fit into various groups, but these efforts usually ended in failure and disappointment. Between the abuse and financial pressures, she found a few things that helped her relax and one of them was finding a bargain. She was as thrifty as she was manipulative and seemed to find inexpensive food at *Gov Mart Bazaar* in the nearby city of Renton, and cheap clothing at *Wigwam* in our own locale. However, being thrifty meant we normally had canned peas, tomato soup, and boxed macaroni and cheese for dinner. Occasionally she would fix my favorite meal, meatloaf. Somehow, she had the right number of spices that produced a pleasant aroma while it baked, and it never needed anything extra when it was served. This dish was firm, yet not dry, and compared to our normal fare, was always welcome.

Several years ago, my counselor asked me to name two things my mother did well. It only took a couple nanoseconds for me to say She made great meatloaf for dinner and oatmeal in the mornings. Even as I said the words, I wept because these were literally the only things I recalled her doing well. That was the first time I was able to share anything positive but even then, the desire to have had more weighed heavily on my heart.

Chapter 4
Music to My Ears

Soon after my final encounter with the major, I became extremely depressed. I was confused by, and angry at, most adult males. Aside from the basketball coach, who was now my PE teacher, I avoided interaction with them as much as possible. When these encounters could not be avoided, my times with them were brief, tense, and cold. But I had no idea that another group of men would soon become like family and provide not only a break from things at home, but also a constructive avenue for my energy and attention for many years.

In the mornings my dad listened to KVI Seattle where we heard news about everything from the traffic conditions to the weather. Although this was not by choice, I gained an appreciation for these types of stations. Most of our friends were glued to the contemporary music stations that played the latest pop tunes. The only times I listened to music stations was while picking berries and at my maternal grandparents' home. During the summers in eighth through eleventh grades, I picked strawberries at Nishimoto Farms in a nearby town and it seemed like someone always had their transistor radio going. The sounds glided gently across the flat, moist ground providing an almost other worldly experience as we toiled in the fields. It also helped me focus on something other than the difficult labor, and it seemed to make the day go faster. Today, when I listen to the ballads from the 60's and 70's, I am immediately transported back to my dried out, and berry-stained, hands, the dampness of the soil in the fields each morning, and the sweet fragrance of the berries.

The only other music I recall listening to was at our maternal grandparents' home every morning we were there. They played the easy listening station with orchestra music and no lyrics. Like the sounds in the berry fields, this remains a *go to* for me when I want to relax and invokes many memorable images of my time with them. Music generates a powerful emotional response and yet, our home had been almost totally devoid of it. This is why the coming change of tunes (pun intended) on my parents' part and how it would impact my life for decades was surprising.

As far back as I can remember, my dad drank eight to twelve *Olympia's* at home each evening but often stopped at other watering holes on his way home from work or immediately after having a few after dinner. Somewhere along the way he met Eric, a man in his mid-thirties, who played the bagpipes. There was nothing striking about him, but he began to come over to drink beer and homemade wine, and just visit with my parents as well as play the bagpipes while standing on our sun deck. His presence brought both a real sense of normalcy to our home as well as hope that things might be turning around. Although he was becoming a regular fixture at the house, I kept my distance from him as I did not trust his intentions. However, his gentleness, coupled with his amazing piping skills, lowered my defenses. Eric became the talk of the neighborhood as the volume made these sessions difficult to hide. I was surprised to discover that although some neighbors were frustrated by the volume, many were curious and seemed to appreciate the piping.

After several months, my dad decided to begin lessons and started playing bagpipes himself. This surprised me as he had never shown interest in music of any kind, and I figured it would just be another thing he did on his own. Anyone who has been around someone learning an instrument knows that the earliest moments can almost drive the listeners insane. It seems like everything is chaotic and lacks any semblance of what one might expect to hear from that specific instrument. I believe that is even more true of the bagpipes! I appreciated that this was a great distraction for my dad and allowed a measure of peace in our home that we had never experienced. It was definitely much easier to listen to his learning the pipes than his raised voice. Before long, we found ourselves immersed into an entirely new, enjoyable, and different culture. For the first time, our family went into public and did not hate the travel to, or from, parades and other performances. It was the only time I recall my dad being truly content and happy. Surprisingly, I was actually proud of him, not just for doing this but also because we were with a group that seemed to enjoy our company. Later, during that same year, I too began to play the bagpipes and others went through the discomfort of listening to me learn this skill.

Each week my dad would take me to Tacoma for lessons on the practice chanter, which I considered an upgraded flute-o-phone because the finger placement was the same as the white plastic recorders we used in music classes at Camelot. Our teacher, Bill Micenko, was a well-known piper throughout the Pacific Northwest. Before coming to Washington state, he had established himself as a skilled bagpipe player in his hometown of Donora, Pennsylvania where, at the age of 16, he became the Pipe Major for the Clan Grant Pipe Band. (Pipe Majors have an important role as the ones in charge of bagpipe bands and establish the sets to be played.) After his audition in 1957, he was accepted as a piper with the Air Force Pipe Band where he continued playing until 1961. During his time in the service, he played for President John F. Kennedy at the Capitol and for Queen Elizabeth while on tour in Europe. After leaving the Air Force, he played with both the *Washington Scottish* and *Clan Gordon* pipe bands before starting a new band, the *Tacoma Scots*, in 1972. Bill remained the Pipe Major until 2009.

Like Eric, it was a joy to listen to him make the pipes sing. He was usually kind to me but had high expectations of his students whether they were in the band or not. He had both a ready smile and infectious laugh but that could change when people had not practiced or continued missing parts of specific sets. And because it was culturally accepted at the time, he knew, told, and laughed at all of the jokes about the *Poles*.

Even though I would spend hundreds of hours perfecting my tunes at home, in his basement, and with the band on Friday evenings, it did not bother me as it was enjoyable. My time with the *Tacoma Scots* became some of the most precious memories from my teen years. I spent hundreds of hours with Bill, and came to know, and fully trust, him. He became much more than just a teacher; he was also my friend. I was relaxed around him, and he helped me balance goofing around or being foolish with tasks that needed to be the focus at any given moment. Our relationship not only helped me move from a depressed state to a positive one, but also helped me trust adult males again. We stayed in contact for many years until I lost his address and phone number during one of our many moves around the United States during my own military career. Unfortunately, by the time I began to reconnect with positive influencers from those tumultuous years, he had passed away. It was a tough day when I heard this news, and my tears flowed freely.

When we arrived for our lessons, I would wait in Bill's living room during my dad's lessons and then go downstairs and begin my own time as the student. After a few months I had demonstrated a firm understanding of the basic movements and was given my first tune to learn, *Scotland the Brave*. I was enthralled with all the grace notes and how differing movements made very distinctive sounds. Sometimes people think learning the bagpipes is difficult but in reality, there are only nine notes with no sharps or flats. The most troublesome part of learning the pipes is coordinating blowing air into the bag and squeezing it when you take a breath. It is critical for the piper to ensure the air pressure remains constant. If this does not happen, the bagpipes become nothing more than an annoying sound. Of course, there was one other aspect associated with playing in a pipe band that was equally difficult, at least the first few times, and that was wearing a kilt. I worried that people might laugh at me and, before going to the car for my first performance with the band, I was as nervous as a cat in a room full of rocking chairs. While some did snicker, most saw it as a tradition being carried on, and once I realized how many were participating in these traditions, it was not an issue.

While I was taking up the pipes, Jim was learning to play the tenor drum. This meant that he, dad, and I were together whenever we practiced or performed with the band – something that was quickly becoming a major part of our family's life. Pipe bands have three types of drums, the bass, snare, and tenor. Each has a unique place, but the best part of the tenor drum section was the twirling of their drumsticks in complex, choreographed, movements. Whenever I watch pipe bands today, I still think of the smile on Jim's face whenever he performed. Like Bill, the gentleman who taught Jim how to do these movements became a friend he was comfortable around. Both of us had found a real place of peace.

Our band practices were on Friday evenings in Tacoma, at the Charles Wright Academy. Like most pipe bands, the winters were a little slower but the spring through fall seasons were a bustle of performances, parades, and competitions throughout the Northwest, in British Columbia and south to the Santa Rosa Highland Games. My sister was not involved in any aspect of this new community, and, for some reason, my two younger brothers became Scottish dancers, when at the time, few males were involved. Neither was ever offered the opportunity to take up an instrument and play in the band. What was quickly becoming a major positive hobby for Jim and me, never materialized for the other three, and that still brings sadness to my heart when I think too much about it. Both Jim and I loved our new roles and continued to grow closer to one another. We also came to understand that these people cared about us. As I began to compete in various piping events, I won several awards but, like with strategy games, my dad quit piping as I continued to improve and develop my skills. Once again, like a morning mist, that disappears in the sun's rays, the opportunity to do something together began to dissipate. Instead of playing in the band, it became another group of friends with whom he could drink, and his responses returned to what we had known for so long. Although he took us to the practices, we were severely reprimanded if we made mistakes. Fortunately, Jim and I enjoyed what we were doing and did not mind when he assigned extra practices for us. Dad never liked the idea of being outperformed by any of his children and seemed to relish the idea of putting blocks in our paths. I wished he could have enjoyed the fact that he was the one who opened the doors to the best part of my entire childhood.

During my 8th – 12th grade years, many of my spring and summer weekends were spent at highland games throughout the Pacific Northwest, playing in parades, and performing at venues. When I began playing with the actual band, it consisted of only adult and teenage males. However, while I was in high school, a few females begin playing the pipes and various types of drums. I spent a lot of time with the three people that were closest to my age: Dylan, Dave, and Georgia. I often clowned around and rarely took things seriously, but they were patient and kind to me. Of the four of us, I would say Georgia was by far the best piper and she did not seem to have an ego that needed to be stroked for her to feel good about herself. She was a very accomplished Scottish dancer as well and was respected throughout the Scottish community. Unfortunately, I often tried to take the spotlight due to my immaturity and insecurities. While the adults sometimes had to bring me back to reality when I was goofing around or not playing correctly, seldom did I take it personally because I knew they genuinely cared about me.

It was during those beginning years in piping that I recognized the fact that if you are good at something, those in charge will put up with a lot of things. Over the next six years of playing with the band, I only recall three incidents where Bill Micenko pulled me aside for serious conversations.

Two of those times he simply expressed his disappointment with me. That was all it took for me to respond correctly as I wanted his approval. The third episode occurred while we were at a quartet competition. My actions cost us any opportunity for placing and brought me face to face with a teacher who was not only disappointed but also angry.

One of the important parts of playing any instrument relates to a sense of timing. For whatever reason, I have seldom been able to just read music and find the beat unless I heard the tune several times. It was always much easier when the whole band, and especially the drum section, was playing and I could almost be on autopilot. However, in solo or quartet competitions, there were no drummers to keep that rhythm going.

Prior to this specific contest, I was given an opportunity to play my pipes for dancers while they participated in a Scottish dance competition in Seattle. I knew the tune, and it was my chance not only to shine, but also get the attention I craved. However, my timing threw all of the competitors off. I was totally oblivious until I was "offered" a chance to take a break and let someone else do it. While I had done my best, without strong leadership in directing and keeping the tempo, I was clearly not able to pull this off. That was why my actions at this particular quartet competition were nothing but self-seeking, immature, and arrogant.

During all of the practices leading up to this event, our focus as a quartet was on the tunes and we played them so many times that our fingers moved with little thought. We were all equal and, aside from Bill leading us during practice sessions, no specific individual would be in charge during our performance. In fact, we were to remain absolutely still. However, on the evening of the competition, as I watched the other groups during their sets, it was clear that one member would keep time with either a slight movement of the foot or by lifting their foot a couple inches in the air and returning it to the floor. When our time arrived to compete, the other three pipers, who were my age with similar experience levels, and I marched into the area adjacent to the judges and then turned to face each other. As we began our set, I decided that since none of us had been assigned the role of keeping time, I would assume that role. It was not because we needed this or because my sense of timing was better than theirs. I just thought it would be cool to be the one in charge – or at least portraying that idea to others.

It failed miserably as everyone's timing was off, the judges could see our precision drop, and the audience recognized my attempts at looking important. Despite my own realization of what was happening, I did not stop the foolishness. I was nervous as we exited the stage because I expected the others to confront me. However, none of them said a word. Later, as we prepared for our several hours drive back home, Bill pulled me aside. He made his disappointment clear and told me that if I ever did something like that again, I would not be playing in the quartet or the band and said I owed each of the others an apology for my actions. His intensity nullified any idea of defending myself or making excuses. I was totally humiliated and the pain of letting him down was real. I did not want to lose the things I found by being part of the band. Unlike my dad's tirades, I knew this moment of reckoning was deserved, and I was in the wrong. Unfortunately, the lesson was not learned from this failure, and I never apologized for this to anyone. It was the first of many lessons, over the next several years, I would have to learn with regards to being humble, accepting my role, and confessing wrongdoings to others.

The following week, when I went to lessons, I noticed something very unusual. Bill treated me just as he had before this incident. All week I had dreaded facing him again, figuring he would still be angry. Instead, we worked on our sets without further recrimination. At band practice there were no comments about my behavior from anyone. In fact, several members came to me and expressed how sorry they were that we had not done well in the competition. Either they had not heard anything or were being gracious. Their responses were contrary to what I deserved but they showed their concern for me. It only strengthened my bonds with them and modeled how we should be gracious towards others.

My years playing with the *Tacoma Scots* taught me much about connecting with people, forgiveness, self-discipline, memorization, and appreciation for different cultures. Looking at pictures from that time always takes me back to specific moments and accomplishments. My time with this group of performers, and friendships I developed helped me through an extremely difficult and confusing next season of life.

Chapter 5
A New World

Becoming part of the Tacoma Scots community helped me develop more confidence in myself and allowed me to finish junior high on a positive note. They also gave me a sense of hope that had not existed when I transitioned from elementary school to junior high. That meant I was eager to become a *Raider* and attend Thomas Jefferson High School.

I wish I could say my home life was also becoming more pleasant, but this was not the case. As I transitioned to high school, my mom and dad's arguments were becoming louder and more violent. His excesses seemed to find new heights and I found myself starting to respond in kind. It was like living two lives, one with the band and at school and another in a house of horrors. My sister also began to have intense arguments with both of my parents. The ones between her and my mom were worse than others as Shelley was called all sorts of vile names, and my mom seemed to try and humiliate her whenever possible. While my mom was normally much less intense than dad, when she went after Shelley it was raw, visible hatred. Things continued this way for months until one day, Shelley seemed to just disappear. Although our paths would cross again in four years, it would be decades before we would reconnect, and I would learn what actually happened that exacerbated the intensity of mom's attacks and her leaving home. Even though Shelley graduated from high school, a great deal of emotional and physical damage had already been done. This would lead her down a dark, painful, and lonely journey for decades before she found a way out. Now it was just the four of us boys in the house which meant there was one less person to absorb our parents' wrath.

At the time I entered tenth grade, there were only two high schools in the area, Federal Way and Thomas Jefferson. While the former was built in September of 1938, our school was built in 1968 and was only about six years old when I began attending. Since it was much closer to our house than the elementary or junior high school, it was easily accessible and I could stay on campus, and out of the elements, longer. In many ways, the school reminded me of Kilo Junior High, but I was surprised to see so many male teachers and counselors. I continued having a fear of adult males, they seemed to accept and respect the distance. This allowed me to gradually open up in their classes, and several became important role models during my time there.

Like all students, the first year was pretty well planned for you. Seldom were students allowed to change classes but during my first week of school one of those changes happened to me. At the time, I had no idea how this would impact me not only during the next three years but also over the last four decades.

Apparently, the English class they placed me in was full, so they reassigned me to a debate class with Mrs. Coe, or CJ as the students on the debate and speech team called her. CJ had already established herself as an extremely capable debate and speech coach, and those who were on the team continually visited her classroom during breaks, lunches, and before and after the actual school day. Like my junior high teacher, Mrs. Maze, it was clear that she cared about her students. She had been teaching for a few years, was both competent and confident, and very laid back. Hanging on her classroom walls were numerous certificates for students who had achieved various levels of success with the *National Forensic League*. After hearing other students discussing tournaments and awards, I went to the main entrance of the school and looked at the large display case. Since I was continually looking for affirmation, it seemed there might be some possibilities with this program. Although I was intrigued by the awards, the expectations of her students made it clear that I needed to change my study habits if I wanted to become a part of the team. My heart was willing, but I had no idea where to get help for what I was lacking. Members of the team seemed to read copious amounts of material and always seemed to be working on assignments for their other classes as well. While they were confident, gregarious, and gracious, I was sullen and cynical, hesitant, and nervous. However, their willingness to talk with, and accept me, in classes helped me overcome my fear of failure or embarrassment. With their encouragement, I approached CJ about becoming a part of this special group of students.

She began working with me individually, helped me develop my first expository speech, and introduced me to the other members of the team. They were studious, but more importantly, very welcoming. Being a member of this team entailed much more than just developing speeches and research; it involved listening to each other's speeches and giving important feedback. This allowed me to learn from some really gifted speakers who gave pointers to improve my developing skillset. Mrs. Coe paired me up with another student, Steve Farris, who would become my debate partner, a great friend, encourager, and a transformative power in my life throughout high school. He remains one of the most intelligent and accomplished individuals I have ever known. Steve exuded confidence in everything he did and was involved in many other school activities besides the debate team. He had a keen mind for math and science and took advanced classes in both areas, was a yell king on the cheerleading squad, and also formed a group he called the *Kaleidoscope Clowns*. Being a year older than me, he had both the experience and confidence to help me navigate this new world. I was shy, so he helped me make connections not just on the team but also throughout the school. Despite my lack of real study skills, he befriended and helped me learn how to make the best use of my study time. Much of this was done through example, as I do not recall him ever lecturing me about these things. He seemed to have the patience of Job - it could not have been easy having me as a partner, especially during those early months.

Over the next two years, Steve and I would spend hundreds of hours together in libraries, at restaurants, on the road, participating in tournaments, eating pizza, laughing, and just hanging out together. His energy seemed endless, and his positive attitude rubbed off on me. He helped me to laugh more and never seemed to be at a loss for words no matter what subject was being discussed. It was impossible not to like him. I never ceased being amazed at all the knowledge his mind could not only absorb but comprehend.

As we prepared for our first debate, there was little time to focus on anything else besides preparation for the tournament, bagpiping, and schoolwork. However, the habits

Steve was helping me establish helped me become more focused in other areas of life. My stress levels dropped as I managed my time more effectively and my confidence grew exponentially.

I came to understand our government, economics, political campaigns, and how taxes impact so much of our lives. A whole new world had opened up to me, and I loved what I was learning. Combined with what I was learning in my Business Law and American Government classes my interests were broadening quickly. I became addicted to learning and reading all I could about these subjects. Magazines like *Time* and *Newsweek* were part of this diet, and they only increased my desire to find out more information. Like the robot in the 1986 classic, *Short Circuit*, I wanted more input and did not seem to be tired when working with Steve. During my freshman year the debate topic was that, "We should significantly change the method of selecting Presidential and Vice-Presidential Candidates." What I learned that year about how we select candidates is still relevant today. People are often surprised when I tell them when, and where, I learned about government and fiscal budgetary issues.

Within a few short months, I had established myself as an active member of the team and began to improve with each tournament. As Mrs. Coe observed me, she noticed I had a quick mind and introduced me to what would become my favorite event, extemporaneous speaking. Oratory, after dinner, interpretive, and expository speeches are written ahead of time and practiced until one can literally do them asleep. However, extemporaneous, and impromptu, competitions allow either limited or no time for preparation. To be skilled in these events, one needs to have read broadly on a range of topics and be able to quickly bring thoughts together into a cohesive manner without a completely written out speech. Then this information must be shared in a manner that the listeners understand and without pauses between words or sentences. It is difficult for some people because the range of topics is broad, and you are put on the spot. I struggled with the impromptu events but quickly discovered that reading a wide array of material about current issues allowed me to do well if I had a little time to prepare. So, I focused my efforts on the extemporaneous events as much as possible but continued doing expository speeches as well. I received my first speech trophy in the extemporaneous events at the University of Puget Sound, and everyone on the team was excited for, and rejoiced with, me.

Most members of the team, including Steve and me, participated in individual speech events and debate competitions. We made a great team because our skillsets complimented one another. At first, I was overwhelmed learning how to debate which involves not only speaking well but also an ability to write copious notes quickly, finding specific quotes to use when it was your turn to speak, communicating with your partner, and putting all of the information into a logical, comprehendible presentation. It demanded every ounce of my concentration to keep up. However, after a couple months, when I discovered how to manage all of the necessary tasks, debate became fun, stimulating. and rewarding. While some freeze if they have to speak in front of others, I found that the nervousness dissipated once I began speaking. My self-confidence grew immensely during my first two years of high school.

Although speaking became much easier for me, there was one aspect of the tournaments that continually caused me concern: my attire and the brief case I had for notes.

When one first arrives at a tournament, a world of chaos seems to engulf you. The hundreds of participants around you exuded confidence and also dressed the part. I had no idea where they found their suits, but when looking in the mirror, I doubted I would be taken seriously. My outfits were of poor quality, mismatched, and normally purchased at second-hand stores. In a feeble attempt to make my attire seem more authentic, I bought a cheap gold chain to make it look like I had a pocket watch in my vest.

Nevertheless, as I participated in more events, it became apparent that clothing really did not matter to the judges. I found them to be fair and impartial, even if I wished they had granted me a win when I had not done so well. The lessons about the value of hard work, coupled with the idea that there were people who applied the rules fairly, changed my perspective on those in authority as well as life in general.

Although I was developing skills that were clearly appreciated by the team, things at home continued to deteriorate. As I became more confident in stating my case about things at school, I was also more vocal about the injustices happening at home. I began to pay a price for questioning my parents as they became even more aggressive towards me. As my dad was became more agitated with me, he began to assault me with more vengeance than before. Jim continued standing up for me and going after him when dad went on his rampages. Because dad was more volatile, his rage seemed to grow even more, and like Jim, I too began fighting back. There were times when both Jim and I would be pulling on his legs, slapping his face, kicking him, or otherwise striking out. Sometimes dad would leave the room yelling and then come back to begin anew once we were asleep. He seemed to realize his control over us was slipping away. This led to his using a new tactic: destroying things that were important to me beginning with the second-place trophy I had received in extemporaneous speaking at the competition at the University of Puget Sound. My reaction was immediate, and intense; I literally pushed him down and screamed obscenities at him. But dad had found something that caused more pain than hitting me. He would use this manner of inflicting pain on me frequently in the coming months and each time it happened, my heart was wounded while the anger and bitterness grew.

My mom began to notice that dad had changed tactics and it was having some effect as I tried to keep quiet when we had arguments. She figured this was something that could be used to her benefit and often threatened to tell dad something, even if it was not true. She would give me a choice of doing something and if I did not respond in the way she wanted, added the comment, "Just wait until your dad hears about this." If this had been about doing dishes or not following the rules, it might have made sense. However, the requests were often related to saying something to one of my siblings so she could see how they would respond or to tell her what they were saying about dad and her. Basically, I was asked to become the family snitch. I hated the whole idea of this and what little relationship we had quickly dissipated. This was when, in my mind, she ceased being my mom and became nothing more than an enemy.

I wish I could say that my attitude was pure and my anger righteous, but they were not. In fact, years of abuse had meant bitterness, malice, and hatred, ruled my heart and tongue. I did not want it to be this way and wrestled with guilt about my responses. However, I felt powerless. Somehow, I felt there had to be more in life. I was becoming a real Jekyll and Hyde as one side came out when I was with Steve and other members of the team, at school, or while piping and the other appeared when I was facing my parents. Even when physically fighting back against my dad, I begged for him to stop because I could not believe he hated me, or any of us, that much. Trying to maintain two different lives took its toll on me. While I was doing well in piping and debate, I was crumbling on the inside. The battle against this darkness inside me was increasingly more difficult to contain. I made the decision to begin getting back at my parents and some of those who intentionally made my life difficult. There was no way I could know that because of my actions, I was approaching an important crossroads.

When I reflect on this period of my life, I grieve about where my heart was. The Bible speaks a great deal about the heart. Ecclesiastes 7:9 reminds us that we should "Refrain from evil...," not only so we avoid sin, but also for our own well-being. Jesus himself explained that evil comes from a heart that is hardened towards God. Paul also focuses on the issue of the heart when he speaks of the flesh. In Colossians 5:19-21 he gives one of his important lists that allows us to look in the mirror and see if we are living righteous or sinful lives. He writes that, ".... the works of the flesh are evident: sexual immorality, impurity, sensuality, idolatry, sorcery, enmity, strife, jealousy, fits of anger, rivalries,

dissensions, divisions, envy, drunkenness, orgies, and things like these...." Clearly, he understood that someone who has enmity in their heart, stirs up dissention and has fits of anger, is not following the dictates of Christ. The reality is that for many of us, we have to come face to face with the consequences, or potential for consequences, before we accept and admit that the problem is in our own heart. So, although reflection on these times is difficult, it was also the beginning of a new line of thinking; I was a lost soul who had a darkened heart in need of redemption. Without reaching breaking points at various times in my life, I would not have learned about, or sought, God's grace. The Lord was about to intervene and drive me to Himself.

Chapter 6
New Beginnings

As the battles with my parents raged, it was becoming increasingly difficult to compartmentalize my life. There was no hiding the growing animosity between my parents and me. An ancient proverb proclaims that, "The enemy of my enemy is my friend." This was clearly demonstrated in our home during the late summer and early fall of 1975 as Jim and I were striking back as a team and my parents discovered a cause that seemed to unite their focus and attention on the two of us. Although they were having limited success when we were together, they began to aggressively go after us when we were alone. There were two distinct battles, separated by about four weeks, that would change my life forever.

The first started one afternoon at the beginning of the school year. When debate and speech were not fully up and running, I would attend school and then come home, go to my room, and read. Since my sister was out of the house, I had her old room upstairs. In many ways, I had hoped this might become a place of solace. Whereas the downstairs room was below ground level, the windows only allowed limited light in. However, the upstairs room was filled with natural light and allowed me to lay on my bed and enjoy the warmth of the afternoon sun. I had painted it a light blue, hung numerous Farah Fawcett posters on the walls, had all types of model airplanes hanging on the ceiling, and displayed a couple certificates and trophies that had survived my father's rampages. Next to my bed were piles of library books and magazines that gave me additional insight into the geo-political world around me. I read information about life, other countries, their governments, as well as autobiographies. Like many teenagers, the closed door conveyed that I did not want to be disturbed. However, that seldom mattered to either of my parents. It just gave me a few additional seconds to prepare for what would come.

One afternoon as I was reading a book, my mother opened the door and began screaming while coming towards me. I did not get up and acted like I was still reading, hoping she would get it out of her system. However, she proceeded to literally stand over me while kicking the bed and jabbing her finger into my temple. That got my attention quickly as it was extremely painful, and it was clear she was not going to quit. As I stood up, she pushed me onto the bed, but as I stood back up, I responded in kind and shoved her. She became even angrier but left the room yelling. After a few minutes things became quiet again and I went back to reading. However, she soon began calling me in an almost pleasant voice. She called me to the kitchen and said she wanted to show me something. I found her standing on the opposite side of our inexpensive dining table, arms folded across her chest. Gone were the angry words and amped up demeanor. In its place was a resolute calmness I had not seen earlier. She stated that it was clear we were probably not going to be friends or get along. Check. Bonus points for clearly stating facts. She then explained why the butcher knife was placed in the middle of the table. I had not noticed our largest knife, until that moment. She explained it was time to finish the ongoing animosity and it was to be a free for all. As I watched, she began pacing back and forth on her side of the table and was becoming more animated. By this time, I had become wary and began to closely watch her movements. Something was not quite right. Finally, she said, "Whoever gets the knife first can do what they want to the other person." *Was she serious? Did I hear her right?* As I considered these questions and sought to understand what was actually happening, she lunged for the knife. As she did so, the table began to buckle so I kicked the table leg closest to me. This caused the knife to move towards the buckle. As it shifted towards her, she grabbed the knife and literally began chasing me around the table. With a great deal of fear and anxiety, I pushed chairs into her way to impede her progress. I knew I had to keep some distance between us as she was swinging the knife wildly in my direction. I understood she intended to harm me. She was as determined as I had ever seen her but part of me refused to accept what was happening. My life was in her hands and had I not ran down the stairs, and out onto the yard, I believe she would have stabbed me. She was past the point of reasonable thought. There was nothing but hatred in her eyes and she was moving as fast as her large body could go. I was already on the street in front of our house when she got to the front door. Once she arrived there, she waved the knife and yelled that if I ever returned, she would kill me.

By this time, some neighbors were looking out their windows or staring at my mom yelling and waving the knife. Some of them probably thought, *just another day at the Mayner's*, as no one assisted me. I ran to the school and sat on the bleachers shaking. After what seemed like an eternity, I began walking away from the school but not in the direction of our house. I traveled west to Pacific Avenue, and then turned north. I walked for hours. To this day, I cannot tell you what I was thinking, or why I went that direction. I was literally in shock and needed to escape from the rampage. Where would I go? Who could I call? Like so often before, I ended up calling Steve and he came, bought me a shake at Arctic Circle, and then took me to another friend's house where I remained for several days. When I finally went home, I literally knocked on the door and then ran behind one of the large cherry trees in our front yard. I did this to keep some distance between myself and whoever answered the door. As it turned out, it was my mother. Calmly, she asked where I had been. With trepidation, I slowly moved from the tree towards the house. She turned and walked upstairs, went to her room, and locked her door.

It was almost as if nothing happened and it was only a nightmare, except it *did* happen. From that point on, whenever I went into my room, I blocked the door with my dresser and had thought through how I would defend myself as well as escape. There was little communication between either of us. Like mom, dad seemed to have withdrawn from the eagerness to engage in battles. I do not know if they figured I might go to the authorities or if they just feared they had woken a sleeping dragon. Either way, I was fine with not interacting with them.

Like most patterns in our home, things could be nice for a while, but they eventually began to deteriorate. Towards the end of September my mom and I were going at it again. However, there was one distinct difference, I was becoming increasingly belligerent and aggressive with her. When she came towards me with her finger, I slapped it out of my face.

When she closed the distance, I slapped her, hit her, and did anything I could to let her know she better stay away. My language had become foul when addressing her. Gone were the attempts to reason with her. Gone was the hope of things changing. I was hyper vigilant and living in a mode of self-preservation. I continually took note of her hands and what was around the area where we were. I literally walked in a manner that my back was never turned to her. When I was out of my room, it was like a mouse stealing cheese from a trap. I quickly did what I needed to and then retreated to my barricade. The anxiety was wearing me out and I would wake up at every sound outside my door. I knew things were spiraling out of control but had no idea how to end this feud.

In the middle of October my mom and I were engaged in a heated exchange. As I began retreating to my room, walking backwards, she kept pushing on my chest and hitting me. One of her swings hit me square on my face and I tripped backwards. She began to pour her rage out on me as she kicked me all over my body while screaming louder than ever. I got up and entered my room hoping to get the door barricaded, but both of us were running on adrenaline and had a great deal more energy than normal. Once I realized the onslaught would not stop, I picked up the chair in my room and began beating her with it. I wanted to hurt her. Like her,

I was now totally out of control. Years of pent-up anger began to be released. However, all the commotion had alerted my younger brother. He yelled at me, and I stopped. This is when I realized I had crossed an extremely dangerous line. It would be the first of two times in my life that I wanted to literally kill someone. As I looked at my mom lying on the floor crying, I knew my time at the house was over.

Once again, I began a long walk without anything besides fear driving me. After a few hours I called some neighbors that had become mentors, Pal and Frank, who lived across the street from our house. Although it was already getting late, they drove to where I was, took me to a burger joint, and helped me calm down. They explained the King County Sherriff's were looking for me and that the best thing to do would be to turn myself in. Although I could do little more than drink some water at the drive in, their concern won the day. They drove me to a location in Seattle where one of the deputies said to bring me. As I was taken back to a holding room, all three of us were in tears.

Being placed in a small, locked room, with just a tiny window was unsettling. I had no books or other distractions. I just had my thoughts, which at the time only involved fear. As I looked around the room, I noticed that a screw holding the window in the door was loose, so I began twisting it back in.

I remember wondering what the other kids who had been in that same room before my arrival might have been thinking. Should I be unscrewing more of these and try to get out? I was just too exhausted, confused, and overwhelmed to even consider running. I cried that night as I had not cried before. I was really imprisoned, alone, and without any control of where things went from there. Once again, I called out to God not for deliverance, but asking why this was all happening.

After a while, a gentleman came in to get my side of the story and as I explained more about the context of the situation, he had additional questions. He would leave for a few minutes before returning with either more information or questions. Their facility was full, so they had few options but to return me to my parents and follow-up when the hearing date arrived. I can assure you, the news of going home was not welcomed by me. However, he assured me nothing would happen and gave me a card with a number on it. He said I could call him 24 hours a day if I needed to. When my door was opened and they walked me out to where my dad was waiting, I was physically shaking. I believed this long night was far from over.

Whatever they told my dad seemed to do the trick as he did not say much during the long ride home. As I went to my room, I barricaded the door but did not change clothes as I figured they would try to do something when I was asleep. In the morning, I went to school as normal but could not concentrate so I went to see one of the counselors. We had talked before, and he seemed genuinely concerned for my well-being. He explained how things would work with the hearing and encouraged me to check in regularly with him. In the days leading up to the hearing, my parents and I had to attend counseling together and I once again saw my mother's acting skills. I could not believe that the counselor seemed to be falling for their wonderful responses. Why did they not bring my other siblings in to discuss things and verify what I said? The result was they felt I was an out-of-control teen. I was both angry and confused. I really thought they would help. The hearing actually ended up being more of a meeting between someone in the juvenile system, my parents, and me. With letters of support from Carol Coe, and a janitor at the school, they decided that juvenile detention would serve little purpose for my crime of assault. However, they did something even better; they placed me into foster care!

Many people have had difficult experiences in the foster system. Mine was not to be that way. My foster parents, Betty and Wes, were great people and while I relished my freedom by being pompous at first, they began to parent me. Their expectations were high, and their discipline was fair. When I was out of line, there were repercussions. I cannot say I enjoyed all of it because there were many occasions I did not respond appropriately. To say I lacked respect of parental figures would be an understatement. However, it was not long before I began to see interesting things that piqued my curiosity. One time, they were sitting in bed reading and I walked by their room. As I said good night, I turned and said, "You really like her, don't you?" Wes responded that yes, he did. The next day he said I did not need to go to school as I could go with him on one of his truck runs. During that trip we talked about marriage and caring for a spouse. This is when I realized that while the Brady Bunch was just a television show, couples do not have to attack each other verbally or physically. For me, this was a new concept that was being lived before my eyes. The next year and a half with them gave me great rest from the tensions at home. I still had to spend some weekends with my parents, and everyone walked on eggshells. It was also during this time that my dad began attending Alcoholics Anonymous (AA) meetings and was finally able to quit his drinking. This was something that brought its own tension, but like everything else, I figured it was just a phase. Debate continued being a huge part of my life during the remainder of my junior year and I was becoming even more proficient and confident.

The most difficult thing about not being at home is that Jim and I were not able to connect as often and seemed to move further apart. Like me, his own battles with my parents were intensifying. Just like when Shelley left the home, with me gone, there were now only three kids to absorb all of our parent's outbursts. During the early days when my dad was trying to quit drinking, he was even more agitated. I knew Jim was looking for a way out and had considered joining the Army, but I did not give it much thought. However, during his senior year, he quit school and joined the Army as a medic. At the time, this was fairly easily to do as we had recently withdrawn from a very unpopular war in Vietnam and had also done away with the draft in July of 1973, so volunteers were readily accepted. Jim went to see SSgt Mike Massa at the Army recruiting office. In short order, he was tested, completed his physical, and headed to Ft Benning, Georgia for basic training.

He made it sound like it was a blast because he was able to shoot weapons, throw grenades, and he was safe in a far-away place. What he never mentioned, or I glossed over, was the fact that basic training was not a casual, easy-going activity, and that a lot was being demanded of each individual who went there. I was proud of him when he graduated, and he looked serious in his khaki's. He was later assigned to the

197th Infantry Brigade back where he began his journey in the Army, Ft. Benning. He seemed to enjoy his role and exuded a great deal of confidence whenever we talked. For him, the Army was a place of freedom, and he was happy having money and living life as a single soldier away from Washington. This brought a measure of peace in his life, something I also sought. It was a quality I noticed about many members of the debate and speech team. They were not a contentious group and seemed to enjoy helping others. Individually, and as a group, there seemed to be a deep peace that permeated their lives, and it was something I wished I had myself.

It was only later that I discovered that many of them were active in a ministry called *Campus Life* and in their churches. They were really trying to live lives that reflected their love for Jesus and shared God's love with those around them. I could not help but be drawn to their kindness towards others and, despite my many flaws, their acceptance of me.

In May of 1976, Billy Graham came to Seattle to hold several nights of evangelistic crusades where he explained the redemptive work of Christ. Several friends asked me to go with them, but I kept them at arm's length. While I wanted to understand God, I was content with the occasional Sunday church. This was my repeated response, but they invited me one final time, and I told them I could not afford it. When they told me it was free, I felt trapped and decided to appease their requests. So, along with hundreds of other students, I joined them on the buses that took us to this event.

I could not believe how many thousands of people were at the Kingdome to listen to this man. The music seemed a little old fashioned, but I was instantly captivated by Billy Graham's words. It was the first time I had really considered that I was a sinner. As snippets of my life played in my mind, it was clear that awards and recognition were not really changing anything in my life. I understood that my heart was the real issue. When Billy Graham asked people to come down to the field if they wanted to pray to receive Christ, I ran down the stairs. I was as sweaty as I was when pushing the broom across the basketball court back in junior high, and just as driven. Don Nelson, one of the leaders who rode the bus with us, followed me down and explained that not only was I a sinner, but also that Christ was the Savior. I knew he was right because my feelings about my parents were not kind or loving. I was willing to do just about anything to begin again.

During the ride back to the school, those who had invited me were once again celebrating with me. Although it had been a long night, I met with Don and another student, Eric

DiDomenico, for breakfast the next morning. These two would be instrumental in teaching me to read the Bible and letting it change my heart and life.

My time at Thomas Jefferson would change as Steve graduated in the spring of 1976 and Carol Coe accepted another position at a school closer to her home near Tacoma. Debate would become a thing of the past, but I still was active in the Tacoma Scots, began attending church regularly, and reading my Bible. These three things would be the focus of most of my senior year. While I was growing in my understanding of the Bible, I was also accepting some things at church that would prove problematic in the future. Some of those things would come up throughout my life as I continued in my efforts to follow, and understand, the teachings of the Bible.

I had not regularly attended any church before, so suddenly I had to learn a new language, understand a new culture, and try to apply what I was learning. At one point, the church began a fund raiser to construct another building on the property. After one of the regular Sunday services, the pastor explained they were having a "business" meeting and encouraged people to stay if they could. Like most of those present, I stayed seated. As things quieted down, a screen was lowered at the front of the church, and someone rolled out an overhead projector towards the front of the church. (For those of you who are curious about what that is, think about a PowerPoint presentation but without anything more than a piece of plastic rolled onto two scrolls, a pen that wrote on plastic, and a lighted mirror that projected the information on a screen.) They immediately began going row by row asking each person what they would give to the *faith-promise* fund. People were literally talking about taking second mortgages. This was then calculated, and someone wrote each individual's name and amount on the plastic scroll. I felt trapped and worried as the time was nearing for me to express what I would share. When they asked me, I decided I should say something, anything, as it was clear that *no* would not be acceptable response. So, I readily committed to contribute $100.00. The people applauded as the pastor heaped praise on me for wanting to serve both the Lord and my country. It is embarrassing today, but I relished those accolades and being noticed in the church.

Like almost every high school senior, I began making plans for what to do after graduation. Having been around airshows, and enjoying military things, I gravitated towards these options. Not only did they seem more exciting than college, but the reality was that I would not receive any financial help from home or through scholarships. I also knew I needed to get as far away as possible, as soon as possible, and leave most of what I knew behind me if I was to make it in the world. It was time to begin a new chapter in my life.

Chapter 7
Being All That I Could Be

Having recognized my options were limited, in October of 1976 I began serious discussions with various recruiters. Although I wanted to join the Air Force, they would not accept me due to the assault charges. It did not matter that they were resolved. Just as I would discover many years later, the Air Force did not have as difficult of a time finding highly qualified applicants, but other branches often struggled and therefore offered more waivers.

A good friend in high school, Kasmir Z., was also looking into the military and had asked me about joining the Marines buddy program that allowed you to do basic training and then be stationed together. I considered it but was afraid that I would not be able to complete the training as I was not remotely physically fit person. With both of those options off the table, I went and talked with my brother's recruiter in the Army, SSgt Mike Massa. I had met him many times before, so our relationship was not new, and he understood many of our family dynamics. He was a jovial man who not only had a great deal of experience as an infantry soldier but also seemed to have a similar story to my own. He ran a waiver to allow me to enlist in the Army. As much as I hated talking about anything with my parents, I needed one of their signatures in order to enlist as I would not turn 18 until the end of August 1977. Without much fanfare, or discussion, my mom signed the paperwork and said she hoped this would work out. That was it. No congratulatory remarks. No hugs, tears, or expressions of joy. Instead, there was just resignation that another child wanted to move far away. Although she did not put it into words, I really felt she was sad, but it did not matter to me. In many ways, I was glad that my decision seemed to cause her pain on some level.

On November 16, 1976, I enlisted as a 13 Echo, Cannon Fire Direction Specialist and was guaranteed an assignment in Germany. There were two main reasons for making this decision early in the school year. The first was the reality that the Vietnam era GI Bill was set to expire at the end of December, and it gave significantly more money for college than the new program that would roll out at the beginning of 1977. The other reason was my fear of not having something in place as I knew I needed to get away from Federal Way as soon after graduation as possible. Throughout the remainder of the year, I was required to check in with SSgt Massa so he could ensure I was meeting the standards and could ship out on my appointed date. My senior year was a blur. Besides playing the pipes, I also got to know another teacher, Mr.

Fabry-Long, better. He was the one that made me want to travel to Europe.

In the fall of my senior year, Mr. Fabry-Long was my teacher for a history class that covered WWII through the present. At the time, he was already well into his sixties with little hair, a wrinkled, but gentle face, and round wire-rimmed glasses. He was slight of build and soft spoken, but his words were powerful. Originally from France, he was formal when addressing students and expected the same in return. It was an interesting class because he shared a great deal of history, often from a first-person perspective as opposed to just being from the work and words of others. I was intrigued and asked many questions in his class. His formality, combined with my foolishness, did not always complement each other. In fact, this was how we began our friendship.

During one of the classes early in the semester, he asked me to stay behind after the other students left. He then asked me to have lunch with him and another teacher in his office. When I told him that would not work, he said that was fine, but he would just put *F's* on my assignments, quizzes, and tests. I did not believe any teacher would fail me for not having lunch with them. However, that is exactly what he began doing. I was upset and complained to anyone who would listen. Before long, it was clear that there was little choice but to join him for the midday meal.

The first lunch with these two teachers was awkward, as they talked with each other as if I were not even there. As the lunch period ended, he told me he expected me to be there the next day as well. I was confused. What was the point of all this? I cannot recall if it was the second or third lunch, but I finally asked, "Why am I here?" His response would become a model for me when working with troubled students later in my adult life. Mr. Fabry-Long explained that he, and the other teacher, felt I was struggling to find my way in school and in life. As they shared what they noticed, and knew from other staff members, I was amazed they cared that much about me. Soon, our lunchtime discussions covered all many aspects of our lives. From that day on, I made it a priority to have lunch with these two teachers.

These conversations allowed me to learn he had survived the concentration camps even though the rest of his family had perished. He spoke of the beauty of Europe but also the sadness of his experiences and why he lived, and sought to enjoy, life to the fullest. I felt free to talk about everything with him and the other teacher. In fact, I actually asked about whether he wanted to be with a woman when he was in the camps. He was not embarrassed and shared that when one is starving, survival is all consuming. His answer was direct, and without recrimination or eye rolling. I regret my foolishness in asking the question, but that is how comfortable I felt around him.

These discussions were a large part of the reason I wanted to go to Europe. I wanted to see where he had been, enjoy the Alps, see Paris, admire the music, and enjoy the foods. My times with these two opened a whole new world and I was going to do everything possible to get there. It turned out the US taxpayers would help me in this quest!

Once I graduated, there was only about 24 hours before Sergeant Massa arrived to take me to the Seattle Military Entrance Processing Station (MEPS) for my final in-processing before heading to Basic Military Training (BMT) at Ft. Sill, Oklahoma. MEPS is where people test and take physicals to enter any branch of the military as well as the place the actual processing happens to send recruits to their initial training. Once the paperwork was completed, those of us heading out to BMT again raised our right hands and took the oath to, "… support and defend the Constitution of the United States against all enemies, foreign and domestic." This was, and remains, both powerful and meaningful to me. It would become even more important in the coming years but at the time, I understood it to refer to the next four years.

After congratulating us, we were handed sealed records and then boarded the bus for a short ride to SEA-TAC airport for our individual flights. Although I had flown on small planes, this was my first flight in a commercial aircraft, and I loved it. Any nervousness I had about the coming days was overtaken by the sheer joy of being above the clouds with the radiant sun glinting on the wings of the aircraft. I was lost in my own little world as I felt something that was new and different. I felt…free. I was free from my home and free to begin my own life apart from my family. I was free to move forward with anticipation and hope. Although I did not realize it yet, these feelings were the antithesis to what I was about to experience.

When I finally arrived at the small airport in Lawton, Oklahoma, it was still early evening. The bus to take us to Ft Sill would not come until around 10 p.m. I was frustrated they had not thought the logistics out better. I actually mentioned this to one of the soldiers who was supervising us until they came to pick us up. He listened but seemed to laugh about my comments. As the bus pulled adjacent to where we were lined up, I was surprised to not see any Drill Sergeants. I remember thinking, "Maybe the movies have it wrong." I would soon learn that both my comments and thoughts were noted and way off the mark.

After a short ride, we pulled up to where we would be dropped off. A group of Drill Sergeants were waiting for us and made it clear they were more intense than what the movies portrayed. In fact, they asked about the "wise ass" who had a better method for arriving trainees. Suddenly, I was the focus of several of these energized Drill Sergeants. Like the hundreds of others, I was shocked by the voracity of their voices and constant, in your face, correction. Within a few short minutes we had done everything wrong and were knocking out push-ups or in the *front leaning rest position.* This would become an all too familiar experience in the coming days. Soon, there would be many 'firsts' in my life. Ft Sill was where I saw my first streak lightning storm. It was where I encountered my first water moccasin up close while maneuvering through a stream. It would be the first time I really appreciated the beauty around me and found that just taking in the scenery can make things more bearable. It was also there that I had my first orange and omelet.

On our first morning at Ft Sill, we lined up at the chow hall and, as we approached the front of the line, were asked what we would like. Still being naïve, I ordered things off the list they had posted. When I was handed my food, I explained that my order was not correct. After several sets of push-ups, the Drill Sergeants told me it was, "Time to grow up boy." I still laugh whenever I enjoy an omelet and have since found oranges to be wonderfully delicious but at the time, I was too focused on trying to figure out what I had missed.

Early in that first week, I was exhausted. Why did we have to continually run and march everywhere? It seemed there was no rational reason for much of what we did. I was slow to grasp that no one was really interested in my thoughts about these matters. Being the foolish boy I was, I copped an attitude. Sometime during the second week, Drill Sergeant King pulled me around the corner of one of our training buildings and began slapping me around while emphasizing the rules and need for conformity.

Although part of me was angry at his actions, another part of me understood the rules were made to help us and they had been clearly laid out. There was no personal discipline that was not unwarranted and most of the pain we suffered related to not working together to accomplish assigned tasks. This conversation with SSgt King, was a turning point in basic. From that time on, I began to respond to, and respect, their authority and quit acting like I knew what was best. He had literally knocked a lot of the arrogance out of me.

As the days and weeks began to go by, I found that the daily work outs and regimen were changing me. When I arrived, I could barely do a pull up, make it across the monkey bars, and was usually one of the last to cross the finish line after our 2-mile runs. It was during a physical training (PT) test during the fourth week I realized I had improved my physical training scores significantly and that was noticed by those in charge. They had also seen the change in my attitude as well my high academic scores. I was beginning to thrive in this new environment and was being transformed from a foolish boy into a soldier. However, there was one area I continually struggled, and it was an important part of soldiering: shooting. The simple fact was that I was a horrible shot.

When we were at the range, the Drill Sergeants walked up and down the line shouting out commands and slapping our helmets with a long metal rod when you did something wrong, something like continually missing the targets! Even after numerous outings to the firing range, I had not improved. On a Saturday morning, while others were having a GI Party (nothing more than extensive cleaning of our areas) I was one of about a dozen trainees that were taken back to the rifle range for additional training. We hopped into our assigned pits and then each of us found ourselves coupled with a Drill Sergeant. I was surprised that there was no shouting or slapping of helmets that day. Instead, they were calm and more like regular teachers who wanted to figure out why we were failing so we could become better marksmen. In my case, the Drill Sergeant discovered that I was jerking every time I pulled the trigger. We spent the whole day on the range but by the end, I was nailing the target, and my instructor seemed pleased by the results. Had this individual training not happened, I might have gone down as a horrible shot and been sent home without completing basic.

When I took the final marksmanship test, I only missed one pop up target, and that one was at 25 meters. I nailed everything else that popped up, including the ones at 300 meters! This was the beginning of my love of shooting. We had much the same process with grenades, but that aspect was not too difficult as it was shaped like a baseball, and I was pretty accurate with it. Although we practiced with the grenade launcher, claymore mines, and the M-60 machine guns, we did not have to qualify on those weapons.

About half-way through Basic, a call went out for those who played instruments. While I think they meant trumpets and drums, I let them know I played bagpipes and they were intrigued. In fact, they allowed me to call home and have them sent to me. Once they arrived, I was playing at the front of several formations as we marched to different training areas to tunes like *Gary Owen*. Another time, one of the training officers was having a party and wanted me to play for his guests. So, on a Saturday afternoon, I was taken off base to play at his home. Once I finished, I played some board games with his 16-year-old son, and then the officers wife took us to the base theater so we could watch a newly released movie, *Star Wars*. I can assure you this was fine by me, but it did not settle well with some other soldiers in Alpha 5, 3rd Platoon. When I arrived back to the barracks, I did not understand why so few of them were interested in hearing about my time at the movie when they had been scrubbing all day. It became a bit of a joke amongst us as they realized I was one of the most naïve people they had met and could not be held responsible for not seeing how stupid it was to enjoy time off while they worked. Lesson learned! Once all the final requirements were met for graduating from Basic, I looked at myself very differently than when I first arrived. I was in the best shape of my life, had grown in my personal confidence, believed I was doing something noble, and knew this was the first step towards opportunities that would allow me to move away from the life I had at home. I also felt connected to those who had gone before me. It was an exciting day when we donned our khakis, and I admired the first stripe sewn on my sleeve. I had never been prouder than I was on the morning of graduation. The Drill Sergeants no longer yelled but we continued doing push-ups and had to maintain a military bearing at all times. In a few hours, I would officially be a soldier.

On the day of graduation, parents came from all over the country to see their sons march across the parade field. Afterwards, new soldiers were allowed to spend time visiting their families and going into town. I too had a pass, but I did not feel like celebrating alone so I went back to the dorm and just slept. Early the next day, each of us moved to our Advanced Individual Training (AIT) where we would learn the specific skillset we had enlisted to do.

For most of us, this meant moving to another part of Ft Sill where we would learn how to survey an area, fire the guns, call in the artillery, or do the calculations. Although there was a little more freedom, and the yelling had ceased, this was still a highly structured time of training. I would spend a lot of time in classrooms learning about map and compass reading, the protocols for using the radios, and how to use various codes. I would also need to know how the earth's rotation affected an artillery shell as it flew through the air, and the difference between up and add since they are different when calculating what angle and charge would be needed to get a 95-pound projectile on target.

We were busily taking in all sorts of information, learning to plot targets and positions on charts, and use an early computer called the **F**ield **A**rtillery **D**igital **A**utomated **C**omputer, (*FADAC* for short) to help in calculations, as well as learning to coordinate our efforts with all of the other elements to put shells down range. It was extremely satisfying when you realize your calculations actually worked and the rounds did not go too far or fall short. Because of the amount of trigonometry used in calculations, I struggled at first but began to understand the slide rules and books we used in the process. It was one thing to be able to do the tasks, but it was an entirely different thing to get it done quickly.

At the end of the course there is a final test that must be passed in order to graduate. Unfortunately, I failed both my first and second attempts. I was just too nervous and could not think through everything in the allotted time. This meant I had to speak with the commander. Because both the Marines and Army conduct their artillery training at Ft Sill, it was a joint command and our commander was a no-nonsense Marine officer. However, much to my surprise, he had already looked at my scores on previous tests and knew that I was taking things seriously. The instructors felt I should be given another shot after some additional review. The commander decided to have me help other students for a week and then give me a test at the end of the time. As the week went by, I gained more confidence. At some point, during the latter part of the week, one of the instructors gave me several scenarios and calculations to run. When I was done, he said, "Congratulations, that was your test." He also explained that it was the same test I had taken, but all the calls and adjustments were 90° different than the first two tests I had failed. By not telling me it was a test, I was able to complete the assigned tasks well within the time constraints.

I was given a day to get my things together and begin out-processing before returning to work for a month with my recruiter as a Recruiting Assistant. One of the out-processing steps was going to the pay office to pick up both my regular pay as well as my bonus. My initial excitement about this money was tempered by the fact that the government took over $500.00 out of my $3,500.00 bonus. I also was not happy to see they were paying all that the government owed me in twenty-dollar bills that would not fit into a purse, let alone a wallet. So, I put the money in with my bagpipes and then headed to the airport in Lawton. I was extremely nervous carrying all that money. However, as I looked around the the airport, I realized there had to be tens of thousands of dollars among all of the soldiers sitting, waiting nervously, for their own flights. This made me laugh as I figured everyone felt the same way I did.

As I prepared to go home, I really hoped, and expected, that my parents would see me differently. But I still had many battles to face, and not all of them would be against the Communists in the world.

Chapter 8
To the Cavalry and Calvary

I was glad when I finally arrived at SEA-TAC airport. It would be the first time being at home with a great sense of confidence as well as having completed a difficult process. Although other soldiers on the plane were greeted by family members at the gates, there was no one there to meet me. Once again, I was alone with my thoughts as I went to claim my bags. After enduring the summer heat of Oklahoma (something I would not miss), it was invigorating to stand outside the baggage claim and feel the light drizzle my face and neck. In the past, these droplets would be annoying, and I would complain. However, on that night, it was refreshing.

In short order, a taxi arrived and took me back to my parent's home. I had never possessed literal piles of money before, and the cab driver was extremely happy to have me on board as I paid twice as much as what was owed and told him to keep the change. I was stronger, more disciplined, and much richer than when I left, and I would let everyone know this!

Once I entered the house, my youngest brother, Mike, was the most excited to see me. I do not remember Tony being present, but mom went back to her room while dad laid on the couch watching television for quite a while before engaging me. When I opened the case holding my bagpipes, I literally threw wads of money into the air as Mike began grabbing numerous twenty-dollar bills as they floated down just like being in the movies. I really felt I had arrived and was finally someone, doing something, going somewhere, and who could splurge by helping his brother enjoy the moment as well.

The laughter dissipated when my dad came into the kitchen. He made it clear he needed to talk with me alone. I fully expected to hear, "Son, I am really proud of you." Nope. Any resemblance to an episode of the *Walton's* or *The Brady Bunch* would have been accidental. Instead, my dad wanted me to know that he had made the decision that I needed to pay rent, food, gas, and mileage for the car I would be using to get between home and the recruiter office. Even as I write this I still chuckle as I was not sure if this was pre-planned, or if he had noticed lots of money floating around and wanted a piece of the action. Any joy I had vanished. It was clear that little had changed since my departure for basic training. During the next couple of days, I visited with a few friends, checked in with the recruiter, and went to church. It is the latter that added fuel to an already warped view of giving at the church and would cause larger issues in the following years.

On my first Sunday back home, I went to church in my military uniform mainly because I wanted the attention. In my arrogance, I wanted others to know they were now safe with me in their Army, looking out for them. I also wanted to give the pastor the money I promised, but I had a surprise for him. As we chatted before the service, I wanted him to know that I would not be giving $100. When I said this, his entire demeanor changed. His jaw tightened and his eyes narrowed, as his face reddened. He was not pleased with me until I stated I would give $300 instead. Once I said that, his attitude went back to being the pleasant, jovial, pastor we saw up front. I purposely set this conversation up and had a feeling where it would lead, and it unfolded almost exactly as I envisioned.

After doing the normal announcements, but before the offering, the pastor had me come on stage where he spoke about what a godly man I was as I was sacrificing so much for God and country. He went on to talk about our earlier conversation and then used that as a springboard to encourage people to be, "led by the Lord" and give sacrificially, just as I had done. There was applause as he finished his prayer and I returned to my seat. When I completed my work at the recruiting office on the following Wednesday, I went to an upscale men's clothing shop and had a custom suit made. It was wool, had a vest, and tailored to me. Of course, I needed a few ties, shoes, and even socks. When all was said and done, I left there having paid a little over $350. While it might not seem like much now, that was a large sum of money in late 1977. In fact, in 1978, my annual pay was less than $3,000!

During the following three weeks, I was the pastor's guest at two dinners in upscale restaurants where he had me share how the Lord had "moved" me to give so generously. I did not feel out of place as I had my amazing suit that established that I was a gentleman worthy of such things. This was followed by his seeking commitments of more money from whoever had joined us for dinner. At the time, I was focused on being treated special as the current feature in the church. I did not know enough to be embarrassed and upset that all of these restaurant bills were taken out of a fund at the church. It would be another year before I had any idea this was not the best practice for a church, pastor, or life.

While on Recruiting Assistant duty, I enjoyed visiting some friends, going back to the high school in uniform, and throwing money around like candy at a parade. However, home was becoming increasingly hostile, and my dad raised my "rent" and mileage fees. Sometimes I think he should have been an entrepreneur as he was surely finding great ways to obtain additional funds from me. Although I was supposed to be in town for four weeks, when I explained my situation to SSgt Massa's supervisor, I was granted approval to be released a week early so I could travel to my first duty station in Germany. I did not tell my parents anything about leaving earlier than planned until my mom noticed me packing. Just like when I left for the Army in June, there was resignation on their faces.

When it was time to take the next step in my Army adventure, Sergeant Massa again came to pick me up, but this time he took me to SEA-TAC where I would begin my new life in Germany. The flight between Seattle and Philadelphia was uneventful, but due to extremely heavy fog, our flight from McGuire AFB, NJ to Germany was delayed for a day. When the time came to go, I joined hundreds of other service members and their families heading to Rhein-Main Air Force Base in Frankfurt Germany. Once there, we would complete our in-processing before spreading out to various bases throughout Europe. I do not know what everyone else was feeling when we arrived in Germany, but I was excited. We remained in place for a couple days and were given limited privileges to leave the base. Being the naïve young man that I was, I paid for everything with American dollars, even though the exchange rate was over two marks for every dollar. When

I consider how many thousands of young soldiers came though that airbase, I am sure the Germans living around that base did very well for themselves!

I took in the clean streets, and enjoyed all the smells of different foods, and knew this would provide some great opportunities over the next two years. Once I received my orders, I headed about 212 kilometers (130 miles) east to Howitzer Battery, 2nd Squadron, 2nd Armored Cavalry Regiment (Howitzer Battery 2/2 ACR). During the Cold War, units of both the 11th Armored Cavalry and 2nd Armored Cavalry provided guard and surveillance duty on the German and Czech borders, respectively. This unit was made up of "H" Company, the armor element with seventeen M-551 Sheridan's that fired a 152mm tank round, Howitzer Battery with its six M-109's that fired a 155mm round weighing 95lb up to a distance of 18 miles, as well as a maintenance and command sections.

Our route from Frankfurt to Bamberg was scenic, and I was captivated by everything I saw. But when we arrived at the base, I was a bit underwhelmed because our unit was situated on a much smaller base across from the 1st Armored Division. In short order, each of us finished our in-processing and then went to our assigned rooms where the teasing, pranks, and trying to assess each of us began. What were supposed to be four-man rooms held a minimum of six and, with all of the requisite gear, the rooms were less than spacious. My room was occupied by an African American from Detroit, a Filipino, two Native Americans, one from Iowa and the other from Puyallup – which is just south of where I grew up, and two Caucasians. Although I was initially overwhelmed by the intense teasing, it was clear the guys were just having fun and meant no harm. Our room held the 'brains' of the artillery, as we did all the calculations while most of the other rooms housed the gun bunnies – those that did all the actual work with the rounds from setting fuses, getting the charges, and actually firing them down range.

Once I stowed my few belongings and uniforms, I crashed on an empty mattress but was awakened by lots of noise around 0500 as everyone prepared to participate in the morning PT. The cool and heavy fog seemed to permeate our PT attire and chilled us to the bone. In my naivete, I really did not consider that this piece would become a major part of my life as a soldier. I believed it was just a part of the initial training. Looking around at the muscular guys around me, it became clear that I met the entry level standards but would need to bulk up to be part of this group. While it could be extremely cold in the winter months, and hot in the summertime, PT provided its own joys of being, and suffering, together, singing cadence, and pushing each other to do better. I came to love these times. In fact, within a few short months, I was significantly stronger and faster than I had ever been and was playing on the unit's rugby team. While I am not a big guy, and therefore in the scrum, they discovered I was a great sprinter and utilized me as one of the backs. This gave me additional confidence and allowed me to participate in soccer and deck hockey for many decades.

Immediately after our PT, we had time to clean up, get the rooms and our uniforms ready for inspection, and have breakfast. Because we were such a small unit, our chow hall only held about fifty at a time so each of the units rotated through on a schedule. However, the cooks got to really know you and what you liked. Further, when you asked for something, you actually got to enjoy it!

Every morning, immediately after breakfast, we had in-ranks inspections where our uniforms and appearance were checked to ensure everything was in accordance with regulations. I quickly realized you could make a lot of points with the senior Non-Commissioned Officers (NCO's) if you put a little extra effort in preparation. This assessment was followed by maintenance on vehicles, sweeping the tank ramps with push brooms, fixing radios and generators, replacing tracks on vehicles, practicing your skills, cleaning weapons, and doing what seemed like menial chores to ensure everything was ready should the *balloon go up*.

This phrase had historical significance because in WWI, when the balloons went up, it was to manage the battlefield with a better view and direct ground troops. What I came to realize is that the whole point of all of this is that wars often begin with little notice, and things needed to be ready to go at all times. Further, even in peacetime, soldiering takes a lot of strength and stamina as you are running around, often with little sleep, while missing meals, repeatedly lifting heavy items, and helping one another. If any piece fails, it literally could mean the difference between life and death. For me, it became part of my personal ethos as I felt, and still feel, we were part of something important. I had a sense of pride in what I did, but it sometimes was too much and became arrogance on my part. While these duties were important, the real tests came when you were out in the field practicing your skills.

One of the things anyone who has spent time in the field can tell you is that it is not always comfortable, easy, or fun. In fact, it sometimes wears on you and frays your nerves.

Shortly after arriving, we went out in the German countryside and woods to establish our initial positions. Riding in a noisy M577 Armored Command post that reeked of oil and diesel, meant we were constantly thrown about as these vehicles were not built for comfort. They were utilitarian and packed with all sorts of safes, communications equipment, charts, maps, personal gear, and C-Rations – the forerunner to the current MRE's the military uses. As I looked around, I could not believe people were actually sleeping while being tossed like rag dolls. About an hour after leaving the post, we began setting up our camouflage netting to prevent – or at least reduce the chances for – unwanted attention by those looking for us, establishing a perimeter, checking radios, and then waiting in position. Sometimes we would be in these positions for a few hours, while other times found us there for a couple days. Whereas we did not carry port-a-potties, that meant we needed to do natures business in the most primitive of ways. It sounds easy, but when you have all your gear on, are wearing a chemical protection suit over your uniform, and really need to go, it can be difficult to try and straddle a slit trench and do your business. Often, one is doing this in the snow and rain. The rest of the stuff seldom troubled me as I enjoyed, and was becoming proficient at, my role calculating data and getting it to the guns to fire their rounds.

Even without actual targets, we were continually drilled as simulated fire missions came in. We made our calculations, the gunners pointed their 155mm cannons in the right direction and ensured their angles were correct, and then simulated the actual firing of said weapon. We were continually timed and there was a lot of competition amongst all of us as our leaders observed, checked, and noted our progress and the areas where we struggled. After several of these, you get the routine down and get into a rhythm. I actually loved being in the field, anywhere out of the garrison really, because it allowed us to do things beyond the normally boring tasks associated with maintaining a small base. As a Private First Class, I was low on the totem pole and had to do all the menial duties. However, those things also motivated me to continually improve so I could be promoted.

Often, we would be traveling somewhere when a simulated fire mission was radioed in for us to give immediate support to a unit in contact. This meant we had to perform what was called a *Hip Shoot* which is basically to deploy all the guns in a field and get rounds downrange as soon as possible. These were stressful moments as everything needed to happen fast and everyone knew it. Unfortunately, I learned about this the hard way one morning as I was handling the radio traffic while we were on the road, traveling to our next position, when the call came in. Without thinking, I said, "Negative, we are unavailable." Suddenly, for some reason, there were many high-ranking people identifying themselves by their call signs and they seemed more than a little agitated. When we arrived back at the base, I was able to have some one-on-one time with our commander and the First Sergeant, the most influential NCO in the unit. I can assure you that mistake never happened again and I was teased incessantly about it for the remainder of my time in Europe. One of the things that surprised me when we did this maneuver is that many kids from the German towns showed up to watch us be soldiers. Like those before us, we gave them all sorts of trinkets and snacks while they enjoyed watching us going through our drills. They normally made us laugh with their antics and I think it was not just me who enjoyed seeing them around. Although each of us had different reasons for enlisting, their presence reminded me of why I was in Germany in the first place.

Another part of soldiering is heading out to actual maneuver areas to fire live rounds, practice on different weapons, and fine-tune our trade. For us, that meant traveling to Grafenwöhr and/or Hohenfels, where we would spend weeks and months living in the field. These training maneuvers were broken up into several day segments before you went back and had a day of maintenance on vehicles, did laundry, enjoyed a hot shower, and were allowed to relax.

Once everything was back in shape, we headed back out and practiced some more. For me, Grafenwöhr became like a second home. However, it was not my only second home while in Germany.

Shortly after my arrival, another soldier, John Ryken, invited me to a Christian Serviceman's Center, operated by *Overseas Christian Servicemen's Centers* (OCSC), which is now *Cadence*, that was near the base. A couple named Paul and Beryl Metko were responsible for the running of the house and working with soldier's along with their three young children, two girls and a boy, and Mrs. Metko's mother, who everyone called Grandma. The children brought a lot of life to the house and seemed to help most of us focus on others as opposed to ourselves – something I was just beginning to learn. There was also a young man, Tim Abbott, who lived there and helped. We hit it off quickly as he was relaxed but really wanted to help me grow in my faith. At the time, I did not understand Paul or Beryl who were the total opposite of what I would normally be drawn to in almost any other circumstance. They were humble; I was brash and arrogant. They were unselfish; I was totally focused on myself. There was a real sense of calm in all they did, but I was a whirlwind of activity.

During the first few visits I was unsure about the Bible talk and singing that went on at *The House*. However, they also coordinated trips, game nights, and meals, and had bunk rooms for those of us who had time off and wanted to stay and enjoy something other than the barracks life. It was not long before I realized that these people were really living in community and were serious about their faith. I enrolled in some *Emmaus Bible* courses and began looking through the Scriptures for hours each day. The more I read, the more I understood. It was clear that I was a long way away from what I should be doing as a follower of Christ. Memorizing copious amounts of Bible verses, using the Navigator's memory cards, began to shift my priorities. Although I was now reading books about Christianity, and seriously trying to live my faith, the real growth came by spending time studying, and meditating on, the actual Bible. My time in Bamberg was when I really put down roots in my faith and discovered that only through time in the Word is there ongoing growth. Further, I had a clearer picture of what it meant to follow Christ because of the way the Metko's lived their own faith.

One of the ways Paul mentored me was through his making time to listen to me and really get to understand who I was not just as a soldier but as an individual. I had a myriad of questions about things that I did not understand - things like someone needing to die by crucifixion, the end times, Leviticus, and Revelation. In his soft-spoken manner, he helped me to not only learn but also to apply truths we discussed. At one point, the church I had given the "offering" to, before heading to Germany, sent me a letter explaining that I had not sent any money that year. I should give them credit for being thorough - they did their research on what I made as a PFC and made it easy for me to know how much I owed them, 10% of my pay. I knew the military was serious about soldiers not paying bills and, quite frankly, I was more concerned about that than what I might "owe" God. Because I talked with Paul about my personal struggles as well as the Bible, I showed him the letter. He helped me draft a response to this church that was respectful, but firm, about my not owing anything. In fact, it was through this process that I learned about giving to the local church, and for me that was to *The House* while I was stationed in Bamberg. That discussion helped me sort through my priorities. It also has been something I have often shared because it really is part of my following Christ. While I have learned to share with the local community of believers, I also discovered there were many solid non-profit groups that could also be supported through giving of my resources.

When I was not in the field, and did not have duties at the base, my time was spent at *The House*. They took us on many trips around Europe and most of these locations were historical cities where we camped, enjoyed food and museums, and immersed ourselves into new cultures. Most of these were enjoyable times and experiences, where I took numerous pictures, and connected with soldiers who did all sorts of work in the Army. However, one of those trips was different than most, our visit to a concentration camp at Dachau.

Having heard Mr. Fabry-Long's story of being a prisoner in one of the camps, I wanted to see what it was like to be a prisoner there and understand more about this ghastly part of history. What began as an interest in another person's experience became one of the most emotional times of my life. I was able to maintain my composure until I touched the empty beds. Thinking about the thousands of people, like my teacher, had been here and either died, or lost friends and loved ones, was too much. I asked God why there is so much suffering and pain. What purpose did all of this have? When it came time to board the chartered bus for the trip back to Bamberg, I rode in silence. My emotions were raw as I considered all that I had and how difficult it must have been for Mr. Fabry-Long to exist in a setting like this. What could I say? It was not enjoyable. Pictures would have been inappropriate, a desecration, as they were not images you would want to hang on your wall. Aside from a small book, I have no physical souvenirs from Dachau. It was a time to retreat, close my eyes, and ensure I did not have to talk with anyone. It was also another reminder of how vile some people become given the right circumstances and rhetoric.

Most of our outings were not like Dachau, and we made great memories, and stories. I came to enjoy the annual conference held with all of the *Hospitality Houses* from Germany, Spain, and Italy. This gathering took place in the iconic Swiss town of Beatenberg, nestled in the mountains, high above Interlaken with a comfortable feel and little traffic. It was everything I imagined. When the sky is clear, you can even see Mount Eiger, which became infamous because of Clint Eastwood's starring role in, *The Eiger Sanction.*

These conferences were times of rest and spiritual refreshment for military members and their families who, on most days, moved at a fast pace. We heard from excellent Bible teachers, sang, and ate meals together. One of those messages, from 1978, remains fresh in my mind every time I take a shower because the topic was our belonging to *"The Order of the Towel."* It has been a constant reminder that we are called to serve in the Kingdom and what our role is in this life. However, we are not to serve only people with similar views and backgrounds. Instead, we are to consider those who are less fortunate and struggling with the burdens of life. The question we were considered to ask was since Christ has done so much for me, is it too much to reach out and serve others without expectation of any return?

When we were not in teaching sessions, we spent our time visiting the shops in town or heading down to Interlaken for a wider selection of Swiss food and souvenirs. Seldom were we alone; we relished the opportunities to connect with others who had the same mindset within the larger military community. When we returned to our individual bases, the training and maneuvers continued but we did so with encouraged hearts. Forty years later, I am still in contact with some of the friends I made.

My time in Bamberg provided the springboard I needed to move forward, and my life would never be the same.

Chapter 9
Love, Marriage, and a New Assignment

Shortly after returning from the 1978 Hospitality Houses conference, Paul and his family made plans for their summer furlough and their home office began securing additional staffing to cover their absence. Tim Abbott was successful in encouraging his cousin, Melody Gorbet, to come over for the summer as a short-term missionary. She arrived just before the Metko's departed, while many of us were having lunch. All of us chuckled when we saw her as it was early summer, and we were casually dressed in shorts, but she arrived bundled up in her thick coat, scarf, and hat. However, despite our chuckles we quickly realized that she was an attractive, single, American, gal.

Like the others, I was thinking about how I might be able to show her around the town – you know, a ministry of sorts! Soon, another couple, Geoff and Sue Parr joined this interim team and become just as special to me as Paul and Beryl. Shortly after the Parr's arrived, there was a parade down the street adjacent to the *Hospitality House*. When I saw it, I went outside and announced to everyone that they must have realized I was there to have all the fanfare. Being a keen observer, Melody stated plainly that I, "… was the most conceited person she had ever known." Of course, I thought she just had no idea who she was talking to as I was in the 'real' unit, doing real missions, guarding the Czech border. Had I said this aloud, it would probably only have reinforced her views and consternation. I left the House that day thinking, "This gal has a lot of spunk!"

By this time, I was reading copious books and articles about living as a follower of Christ, and also spending a lot of time in the kitchen helping prepare meals for all of us. I enjoyed being part of this family group and came to enjoy creating things from recipes. After her arrival, it also allowed me a lot of time to be around Melody. Although our first real interaction was anything but positive, it was clear that she was seeing my heart for God and, ever slowly, changing her view about me. We spent many hours talking, laughing, and doing dishes. I was impressed by her faith and commitment to following Christ as well as her genuine concern for others. Sometimes that concern was not easily seen as she often had a very serious poker face that was hard to read.

Jeff, Sue, Tim, and Melody all spent countless hours modeling Christ before each of us who came to the *House*. They challenged us to make Him a larger part of our hearts and lives. They were encouraged to see my growth and serious studying – I was taking things to heart and not always goofing around. Further, the more time I spent talking with Mel, the more she became a major part of my week. Unlike two other girls I was seriously interested in during high school, but did not develop any relationship with, I wanted to get to know t Melody but had no idea how to proceed. At some point I shared these thoughts with Tim, and he let me know it would never work because she was almost five years older than me, had already graduated from college, and came from a strong Christian home, not to mention we were so different. That conversation cooled my jets for several months, but she never really left my mind.

As the summer drew to a close, Paul and Beryl returned, and Melody was approved to remain on staff for an additional nine months. Things were back into the normal rhythm as the seasons changed from fall to winter. Then, early in January I had a pain on my lower right side that resulted in me being rushed to the military hospital in Nurnberg. The doctor performed an emergency appendectomy after which I was taken back to the barracks and put on light duty for a week. At the same time, people at the *House* noticed I was not there, and Melody realized she really missed my humor and our conversations. When she found out what happened, she wrote a card and had one of the soldiers deliver it to me. More than anything else, this motivated me to get back on my feet and back to the *House*. I was excited that she had noticed my absence, and it was a genuine act of kindness that showed me that she really did care about me. A couple weeks after this, we all traveled back to Beatenberg for the annual conference. During one of the sessions, we were singing various Christian songs but then transitioned into a silly song about grabbing the hand next to you. I had not planned this, but I was sitting next to Melody and, suddenly, we were holding hands, and I was turning beet red. As our hands touched, we both looked at each other and smiled. However, the next verse had us swinging the hand next to us and, as we locked eyes once again, I smashed hers into the wooden chair in front of us. Although it was a little painful, we both laughed the way nervous boyfriends and girlfriends do when they realize that the feelings are mutual.

After the session ended, I asked if we could talk. We walked to her room and, while standing on her balcony overlooking the Alps, I expressed my feelings about her. She too shared that the feelings were mutual, but it would complicate things because when accepting the position, she had agreed not to date any of the soldiers. In fact, an officer had already asked her out and she explained the same thing to him. Just knowing she felt many of the same feelings I did was an encouragement to me but I did not want to cause her problems so I figured we would keep things as they were. After a few more minutes, I went out with other guys to go sledding and play around in the snow.

Once we returned to Bamberg, one of the other soldiers, who was married, asked me if I wanted to go bowling after chapel. We were both from the Seattle area, and discovered our dads worked together at Boeing, so we had become fast friends' months before and it seemed like a fun outing. As we went to their car, I noticed his wife, Janice, had someone else walking beside her. It was Melody. I began to blush and was too tongue tied to say anything. After a few awkward moments we all laughed because, without knowing it, I had talked with Carl about the situation and Melody had talked to Janice. They wanted to help us out by being our chaperones on what would become our first real date. This cemented our friendship with both them and one another, but I have never bowled worse than that afternoon.

At some point during the following week, while alone in the kitchen with Melody, I asked her to close her eyes. She was hesitant but decided to humor me. When her eyes were closed, and I was sure everyone had gone to the large room for singing before the study, I kissed her. However, I was too scared about what she would say so I quickly said my goodbyes for the night and headed back to the barracks. I knew there would be questions from the others about why I was not staying for the study, but I was embarrassed and not sure how Mel would respond later.

Surprisingly, she was happy about what happened and let me know that despite the problems this might create, she would discuss the change with Paul and Beryl. I wish I could say everything was wonderful, but this was new territory not just for us, but also for Paul and Beryl as well as the organization. They could not have jealousies among those who attended the *House*, but I did not understand why there was any concern. We were both adults; right? Well, one of us was an adult while the other was an impulsive, immature, pimple-faced 19-year-old.

The situation was concerning enough that the gentleman in charge of the ministry in Germany, Dick Patty, spoke with both Mel and I individually. He tried to be graceful and pointed out the many areas of concern. He spoke to us about difference in ages, my young (but growing) faith, and the short time of knowing one another. As I look back on these conversations, I have to laugh because when Dick said I was immature, I responded, "Well, give me a maturity test then!" I did not know it at the time but once I said this I already failed.

To their credit, they agreed to allow us to see each other but it had to be during her days off, we could not hold hands or show any other outward signs of affection while together at the house, and we were not to be alone at the *House* or while on any activities sponsored by OCSC. We agreed, but these rules created a different set of issues in the coming days.

It was difficult to keep our relationship under wraps in a small military town. One afternoon, another soldier, who was a regular at the *House*, noticed Mel and I walking hand-in-hand. Soon it was clear that we were a couple, and the secret was out. After some initial misunderstandings, Paul and Beryl shared that they had asked us to be discrete and prudent in our actions and activities so as not to interfere with the ministry.

After only seven months of knowing her, I asked Melody to marry me. However, unlike the movies, she told me she would, "think about it." What? I thought I misunderstood but also knew she had been engaged once before and had broken off the engagement. She told me that this time, if she said yes, she wanted it to be firm and not waver. So, after about a month and a half, on April Fool's Day (I always tease that this was so she could tell a judge it was all just a joke), she said she would marry me.

Since Mel would only be in Bamberg until July, we spent more time together, but with others knowing about it, things were much easier as we did not feel like we had to hide from everyone. As July approached, I was anxious about what it would be like when she left. The day arrived when she returned to her home in Escondido and prepared for our wedding, which would take place when I came home in November. As she was departing on her flight, I was overwhelmed with emotion and considered how lonely the next months would be without her there.

The remainder of my time was busy with several trips to the field as well as the normal routines and alerts associated with being in a combat arms unit assigned overseas. Melody and I corresponded daily, and I began writing regularly to her mom and dad so I would not be a complete stranger when I arrived just before our wedding date. I left Germany during the first week of November 1979 and traveled to Mel's home in Escondido, California. After our wedding, we would head to Ft Lewis for my next assignment with the 9th Infantry Division Artillery.

Upon my arrival in San Diego, I was enthralled with the clear skies, gentle breezes, palm trees, and the wonderful smell of the ocean air. Once we arrived at her house, Mel's father, John Q, gave me a hug – something I was neither used to or expected. When we went inside, her mother hugged me, but was a little less enthusiastic. I was exhausted from travel and slept soundly for more than twelve hours before waking up to the sounds of parrots in nearby trees.

What I did not fully understand was that since Mel's church required a specific number of premarital counseling sessions before they would officiate any wedding, the next two weeks would be busier than we planned. In fact, I felt a little like Danny Kaye in the 1956 classic, *The Court Jester*, as they fulfilled all the requisite steps to make him a knight. We spent about two hours each day doing the required premarital counseling and then a couple more completing assignments. It was very clear why their pre-marital counseling normally begins nine to twelve months before a couple gets married. While I am a believer in having frank discussions about various aspects of marriage with a neutral third party before the ceremony, I would not recommend our crammed course. For me, it was a test in patience as I just wanted to get to the "Man and Wife," part! When not attending these sessions, or reading from the assigned list of books, we helped her parents prepare for our wedding.

I had always wanted a larger wedding and, since Melody's parents had a wedding decorating business, it would be grander than anything I could have imagined. Each day I met more of her family, tried to remember names, and repeatedly shared things about myself. Often, they seemed more interested in my playing the bagpipes than getting to know me as an individual. In reality, they were probably sizing me up knowing that they would have very few opportunities to visit before we headed to Washington.

On our way to Ft. Lewis, we spent time in Santa Barbara, San Francisco, Redding, Grants Pass, and Portland. However, within a few short days, many of our differences became apparent. We were now spending time just as a couple without any experience of just being together. We were exhausted from everything leading up to the wedding, and I was emotionally spent because I recognized that Melody's family was very strong in their faith while I was still trying to understand what I was learning. In many ways, I felt out of place and wondered how things would work out. Like most young couples, we made the best of it and believed we would adjust to living with the idiosyncrasies of another individual.

Since making a serious commitment to follow Christ while in Germany, I thought my relationships with my parents and family would be better than when I left. However, things were still tumultuous at best. A soldiers life revolves around preparation for war which means spending a great amount of time in the field. As such, most of my time at Ft Lewis was spent both at maneuver areas on the base, at the Yakima Firing Range and participating in airlifts and exercises at Ft. Carson, Colorado. This limited the opportunities to develop relationships with my family.

When we arrived at Ft. Lewis, my dad had been sober for a couple years and attended AA meetings faithfully. I was proud of him as he seemed calmer, almost pleasant. There were moments when I expected we would do some things together, but he was not able to do so with any of us kids. Instead, we chatted about surface things like the weather, how busy I was, and what the next meal might be. My relationship with my mom was still strained as she wanted to do things with us without addressing some of what occurred over the years. While she also attended AA meetings, I was always puzzled because I could not recall a time she was even slightly buzzed.

Although I was not too familiar with AA, I read that one of the steps was to make amends to those they had harmed. If either of my parents tried to apologize, it might have made a huge difference. Unfortunately, this never happened before either of them passed away. They felt I was arrogant, had joined a cult because I was serious about church, and placed a high priority of living differently. They were correct when they said I was arrogant, as I was still puffed up about what I did, my military awards, and what I believed was right. Unfortunately, I did nothing to alleviate the tensions and would later regret my words and actions that belittled both them and others.

As the date for my discharge approached, I decided to attend Multnomah School of the Bible, now Multnomah University. My parents could not understand this and, in one of the few deeper conversations we had, told me it was a poor choice. However, my mind was made up and I headed to college in Portland.

Chapter 10
Lessons in Faith

After being discharged from the Army, I enlisted in the Air Force Reserve and received training as an Aerial Porter. Although I would not begin participating with the unit for the required one weekend, a month and at least two weeks a year, until we arrived in Portland, it was a great relief to be fully out of the Army.

After spending a relaxing summer in Escondido with Melody's parents, we began our road trip to Portland. Instead of driving the more direct, but boring, route up I-5, we went north via Hwy 395, and stopped at Yosemite. I was in awe its expansive beauty. This was my first experience staying at a National Park and it started my appreciation of our National Park system. The time we spent around a campfire, floating down a slow-moving river, and admiring Half Dome were a welcome time of refreshment as I could not have known how busy my life was about to become. Although Melody had already attended college and I had several friends who had gone through that experience, no one in my family could advise me about this except my aunt. I figured that since I would not be taking many science and math classes, it would be easy. Of course, the reality is that any college program takes a great deal of effort, demands that you prioritize your time, and if working full-time while doing this, leaves you with limited opportunities to rest. Fortunately, I had developed a strong work ethic in debate and refined it while in the Army. The next four years would force me to hone these skills further because I would soon be overwhelmed by all the demands heading my way. Although the GI Bill helped with some of the expenses, it did not cover all of them. Since we had a goal to leave without debt, both Mel and I took full-time jobs to make this happen.

We moved into an apartment in the northeastern part of Portland just a couple miles from the college. Shortly after moving in, I responded to a *Help Wanted* ad for a prep cook at North's Chuck Wagon where I would spend the next three years working as both a prep cook, and then as a lead cook. It was a job I thoroughly enjoyed.

After reading through all the syllabi and required books, tears welled up in my eyes. I did not believe I could do all the required reading and writing assignments while working 35-40 hours per week. However, as Mel and I talked I realized that if I organized my time carefully, it might work. With that in mind, I taped the large, monthly, calendars for the semester on a wall and annotated every assignment and my work hours on them. This allowed me to manage almost every waking minute to the fullest. It was clear that my time with Steve in high school had rubbed off. I soon began to see results and my confidence soared to new heights. Although the bulk of my time was split between North's Chuckwagon and college, I also had duties with the Air Force Reserve. Once a month I went to the Portland Air National Guard Base on Friday evening where a C-141 would whisk about 100 Air Force Reservists away to McChord AFB, WA. The flight normally returned to Portland at about 8:30 on Sunday evening. The duty was enjoyable but made for two long weeks of having no days off whenever I pulled duty up north.

At the time, the focus of Multnomah was the Bible and ministry so all of us had similar schedules, assignments, and eventually had most of the faculty as a teacher. This also allowed us to develop friendships because we spent a great deal of time studying together. Looking back, I realize how those relationships changed the direction of my walk with Christ.

Alan MacLurg was one of the individuals who has been a friend for over forty years. I met him during our first week of at Multnomah and got to know both him and his wife, Cindy, as the years went by. I have always been impressed by their genuine humility, kindness towards others, and the grace they showed to both Melody and me. Like Melody, they were raised in Christian homes and were strong in their faith. They were soft spoken by nature but competitive when they played sports. However, this was not the hyper-competitiveness I was used to seeing. Instead, they enjoyed a good game but always encouraged others. During the first two years in college, we were part of an informal group of several married couples who shared Saturday brunches together, helped each other when financial concerns arose, and also began our families while there. Our times together were a refreshing break from the rigors of work and classes.

While at Multnomah, I found myself struggling because there were strict rules about conduct that might make sense for a 17- or 18-year-old student living in dorms but seemed a bit over-reaching for married students. I wrestled with the rules because I felt they focused on outward things and did not have any bearing in life. One of the things I struggled with most is that I could lay naked with my wife in bed but could not dance with her. How did the two go together? Other rules included not being allowed to play cards, attend movies, or watch television, none of which seemed too critical to me. Since I signed the agreement(s), I tried to follow the rules, though I pressed the guidelines to the brink of bending.

It was only after being out of college for a few years that I realized the rules were not the issue. Instead, it was a heart that was focused on itself and questioned anyone in authority who I did not respect. Because I felt behind in what others already knew about the Bible and ministry, I often had a poor attitude, was still arrogant about having served in the military, and occasionally used foul language. I could not have completed my degree without the encouragement of my friends. Despite knowing all of these things about me, Alan and Cindy never abandoned us. They never treated us like a burden. Their example would help me come alongside many who struggle in life and with their faith. They helped me see people through God's eyes, respect them as individuals, love them without a sense of superiority, and not expect perfection.

There were also three professors who had a profound impact on my life. The first was Dr. John Moore, my teacher for the *Pentateuch* – which is just a fancy word for the first five books of the Bible. He was a serious Dallas Cowboys fan and had a quick wit, coupled with a serious tone when it came to applying what we were learning. I remember he used the example of Moses and another individual to explain that there might be a line we would cross in life, and the Lord would no longer use us. I was puzzled. I thought God forgave all sin and it was not connected to anything we did, or could, do. This new concept hit me hard because of my earliest years at home and now, my struggle with the rules at college. Because I was still full of anger and bitterness, what did this mean for me? This caused me many sleepless nights. If this concept was true, and I was already disqualified, I had to ask myself why I would spend any more time learning how to live as an ambassador for Christ? I began asking more basic questions about whether I was even saved. When I talked about all my confusion with Dr. Moore, it only created more doubts. By the end of that first year, I was having a serious crisis of faith which led to my going over to Mt Hood Community College for a year between my first and second years at Multnomah. It would be several more years before I was able to resolve these issues in my own mind and find any real peace on the matter. However, the whole experience reminded me that just because someone was a professor did not mean they had the corner on understanding everything they spoke about.

At community college I took general courses but remained in contact with another professor at Multnomah, Dr. Sauerwein. I had him for the second semester Bible Study Methods class during my freshman year. For whatever reason, he seemed to understand I was wrestling with understanding the Bible and applying it to my life. He encouraged my questions and met frequently with me to talk about the assignments and how I was doing. Like Mrs. Williams in elementary school, and Bill

Micenko in the pipe band, he was someone I felt safe around. Dr. Sauerwein helped me discover the art of making Bible passages become clearer by using the first person instead of just reading about others. It is a powerful tool that I have used for over forty years. Today, I automatically read many New Testament passages in the first person. In fact, I do the same thing with songs when I sing them at church or along with what I hear on the radio. My first book, *My Journey in Psalms, a First-Person Rendition of the Psalms and Associated Prayers*, was the next step in using this method to gain a deeper understanding of the Scriptures as I honestly cried out to God for understanding, deliverance, and peace.

Unfortunately, my time at college was anything but peaceful not only as a student but also in marriage. Melody worked during the day while I worked at night, and we seldom connected as a couple. Just as it had been in high school debate, I always wanted to learn more and spent many extra hours reading all sorts of books to gain better insight and understanding of the Bible but did not put the same effort into our marriage.

Once I returned to Multnomah, I arranged my entire schedule around taking the following two years of Bible Study Methods from Dr. Sauerwein. My wife, as well as other students, were confounded by this. However, Dr. Sauerwein was okay with my silliness as he recognized that I was also curious, studious, and wanted to live a more Christ like life while serving others. His classes were always a highlight for me and no matter what I felt prior to his class, I seldom left without feeling understood. He was content knowing that God was at work in my heart. It is one of hundreds of examples where gracious people brought comfort to my heart through acts of kindness.

There is one other professor who I never really connected with but his participation in my life, both as a student and after graduation, would be the springboard to one of the most critical points in my life. Part of the reason for not being able to visit him during his office hours related not only to my working so many hours each week, but also the arrival of our first son, Rob. I discovered that holding him gave me a sense of purpose and joy. I enjoyed being a parent alongside Melody and was able to see her more often as we had made the decision that being a stay-at-home mom was important to both of us.

I was often overwhelmed in the classes because much of the information being covered was totally new to me. Aside from a few activities and programs at church in my youth, I only had the time at the Hospitality House to draw upon. While I became more grounded in my faith while in Germany, I was unfamiliar with almost all of the Old Testament. When it came time to take a required class on the prophets, I was repeatedly told how great Mr. Dave Needham was, so I signed up for his class. Throughout the first week I eagerly anticipated seeing what so many raved about. Unfortunately, at least for me, this never happened. But the reason had nothing to do with his teaching about the prophets. It is true that the amount of reading in the course was astronomical. It is also true that when coupled with everything else I had that needed my time and energy, completing all the assigned reading was more about skimming the material as opposed to pondering it. Mr. Needham's was transparent about his spiritual life, including questions he did not have answers to. He sought to live openly and honestly before us. In doing so, he opened my mind to a whole new part of being a servant of the Lord. It was an arena that I had never even considered until his class.

Where many professors move to the assignments and topics at hand, Dave Needham shared about what he was learning as he read through the passages he was preparing for class. I was awestruck. I could not believe someone in their mid-fifties had not actually arrived and understood it all. I found myself contemplating truths he was sharing instead of taking notes during the class. This led to my only "C" while in college and caused all sorts of frustration on my part. I liked maintaining at least a 3.20 GPA, but that class affected the semester.

Dave spoke with a conviction that I have seldom heard from anyone, and the things he told us were important. He spoke of continually evaluating his heart and seeking to follow the leading of the Holy Spirit. When I graduated, I was happy to be done with his class as it was extremely demanding, and I was never quite able to focus on the lectures related to the prophets. It would be a little over a year before we would meet again and our interactions would lead to one of the most transformative moments in my life. It would be a moment where I felt like God sent a prophet that would speak directly to me so that I would finally hear a message He needed me to understand.

During my senior year it was important that I secured employment since we had a young family. Melody and I applied to become missionaries with OCSC, and figured missions were desperate, so it was just a formality. We were wrong, they were concerned not just about the mission, but also the missionaries themselves. During the appraisal phase they gave us a battery of tests, and I scored high on anger and low on the depression scale. It did not matter that I was probably not on their scale before coming to Multnomah, and it had been years since I hit anyone with an object. No, what mattered were the indications that there were some deep-seated problems. This not only stopped our plans, but also left us without any real options. In other words, I would be unemployed after graduation. I went into a deep depression wondering if maybe God would not use me and if all of the studying and reflection on issues within my heart were wasted time.

This was especially difficult because Mel and I had our first son, Rob, in October 1983. Although our relationship was often strained by working opposite schedules, we made the decision to begin a family and have Mel quit work. The pressure of finances became something that gnawed at my heart almost every day. However, as we took our Lamaze classes and saw the grainy ultra-sounds, the excitement of having a child drew us closer together. It is amazing how quickly Melody's body showed signs of this new life. It was amazing to feel Rob kick and move around. Those precious moments before birth were nothing compared to the feelings once he arrived. I could hardly believe the little boy was our son and was committed to raising him very differently than my parents raised us.

Since I would not graduate until May 1985, Rob would be a welcome relief to the demands of the world. I found that coming home would energize me knowing he would be so happy to see me again. There was something special and relaxing about holding a baby knowing they fully trusted you. I could not get enough of him. Having Melody home instead of her being at work also allowed us to connect at a deeper level.

After graduation, we returned to Mel's parents where we would remain for over two and a half years. Once there, I looked for employment and also transferred to March AFB, in Riverside. Given the state of the economy, jobs were scarce during this time. I dug trenches by hand, drove both school buses and water trucks, and worked at Burger King in their management training program. Although the latter offered substantial financial opportunities, I was not impressed with how rudely the management treated their employees. I decided I could not be part of a program that encouraged the constant berating of the workers, especially in front of customers. It saddened me to see the high schoolers working there feeling like this was how work should be.

However, I soon discovered there were extra *man-days* available for reservists to support the unit's mission. I was able to work hundreds of these 'man-days,' and complete Rigger School at Ft Lee, Virginia. Once I completed that course, even more opportunities opened for me because the unit needed more riggers in order to maintain their proficiency dropping various sized cargo and vehicles. I loved the physicality of it all, helping set up the aircraft, and watching my loads successfully deploy from the aircraft. Part of my enjoyment of the work also related to the senior enlisted Chief Master Sergeant, Larry Wynn. He was, and remains, one of the kindest, self-sacrificing, leaders I have ever served or worked with at any time in the last fifty years. He did not raise his voice, always listened with empathy, and looked out for our welfare. Chief Wynn had integrity like few others I have known and really lived the ethos of *Service Before Self, Integrity, and Excellence*. While I was bringing in regular income through this work and my career was doing well, the same could not be said about my spiritual, emotional, or marital life.

Spiritually I became angrier at God. Emotionally, I felt like a total failure and spiraled into depression. Traveling so much for the Air Force meant I could not be there as a father because I was often gone for weeks at a time. I found little joy in life; I felt like a cog in a machine that was just going through the motions of living. My relationship with Mel also suffered not only because I was absent so often but also because she was not sure how to respond when the times of depression overcame me.

After graduating from Multnomah, I began to question whether God even cared about me or interacted with the world in general. This would become my second crisis of faith. Simply put, I believed God had failed His part of the bargain. I sought to live a moral life, attended church, and learned more about the Bible and was convinced that the Lord would, by obligation, grant me a wonderful job and the American dream. However, this was not a contract God had any obligation to fulfill! In fact, all of it is predicated on a misguided understanding of who He is and what is important to Him. God is concerned about the heart. He does not work in our lives to make us successful in the world's eyes. Instead, He seeks to rescue, refine, and restore people's hearts for His Kingdom.

Somewhere in my journey, I acquired a skewed understanding that needed to be corrected. At the start of the second year of living in Escondido, Mel's sister and husband invited us to Redding, California to attend a Family Camp with their church. We needed a break, so we joined them for the three-day event. When we arrived, I was less than enthusiastic to see that the speaker was David Needham. I was not interested in hearing what he had to say, but I attended the sessions out of a feeling of obligation. After the first session on Friday, we exchanged pleasantries, and I told him I was struggling with a lot of things. After the morning session the next day, he asked me about what was happening. I told Him that God had, "screwed me over." He listened as I spoke loudly and with an intensity that indicated I was frustrated and angry at the Lord. When I finished, he gently said I, "had the wrong perspective." What? Really? I could not believe my ears. The audacity of his fatherly tone did not sit well with me. Since I figured he had not really heard me, I retold my story, using colorful metaphors to help emphasize the parts he seemed to have missed. He then encouraged me to go back and read the Bible to see who God really was. There was no admonishment, just compassion and concern. He understood that what I had believed for so long did not align with the Bible or with the God he knew and trusted. While his words touched me deeply, it was his eyes and compassion that broke me. Once he left, I wept. I cried tears of anguish, confusion, and brokenness. A lot of pain finally came out as the streams ran over my cheeks. It was as if Jesus himself had reached out and touched me. My emotions were raw. I had finally spoken the truth and it showed a darkened, hardened, heart, and I realized my view of God had been wrong all along. It was not because Dave argued a point that this struck me. No, it was the gentle spirit he showed as he spoke the truth. This approach reinforced what I had already begun to learn through the example of Mr. Fabry-Long and Carol Coe in high school, Paul and Beryl Metko in Germany; and Alan, Cindy, and Dr. Sauerwein at Multnomah. These individuals were all about grace, love, and coming alongside those who were lost, hurting, and striking out because of the pain.

After returning from the retreat, I began reading the Bible differently. I was no longer interested in the academic, cerebral, knowledge of the book. Instead, I was actively seeking to know God better. Beginning in Matthew, I read the New Testament with a different goal. I began to notice how Jesus interacted with those who had questions and I was touched. However, it was not until I arrived at Ephesians that the miraculous happened. In Ephesians 1:3-6 I read, *"Blessed be the God and Father of our Lord Jesus Christ, who has blessed us in Christ with every spiritual blessing in the heavenly places, even as he chose us in him before the foundation of the world, that we should be holy and blameless before him. In love he predestined us for adoption to himself as sons through Jesus Christ, according to the purpose of his will, to the praise of his glorious grace, with which he has blessed us in the Beloved."* Did you see what motivated God to do this? I did! For the first time I really understood that God's motivation was not obligatory. No, it was based on love, which also meant, that He loved, and continues to love, me. I could not stop the tears that flooded the pillow as I laid on the couch where I was reading. These were deep sobs of relief and rejoicing. It was as if God had removed a great weight from my entire being and allowed me to commune with Him in a new, and marvelous, way. It was already late into the night and Mel was asleep, but I had to tell her the news. I could not contain my excitement that God loved me. This was no longer hypothetical. I was flooded with a joy that I never experienced before. Understanding that I was loved by the God of the universe was a game changing event that would impact both my heart and life.

Once I grasped this fact, it became clear that my perspective was the issue. If I were to follow the Lord, I knew this had to change. God was faithful and used this discovery to show me that there was still a lot more refining and healing that was needed. Although it would be another year before I secured long-term employment, I was excited to see the Scriptures through this new lens. I no longer just looked for facts in the Bible. This allowed the words to do their great work of conviction, helped me understand more about His character, and gave me insight into His real mission – redeeming hearts and lives from the enemy. By this time in my life, I had read many books by different authors about truths in the Bible. However, I was discovering that the real treasure was not in what others said about the Bible. Instead, it was by reading the actual word of Scripture that changed my heart. Although

I continue reading other people's writings on specific issues related to faith, I spent a great deal more time in the Scriptures. This has proven to be the most powerfully transformative activity that has convicted, encouraged, challenged, and comforted me throughout the last forty-five years.

Chapter 11
A Different Kind of Service

In the months following my discussion with Mr. Needham, I learned of opportunities to return back on active duty as a recruiter for the Reserve. Unlike the experiences of those whose recruiters were not positive, both my Army and Air Force Reserve Recruiters were polite, helpful, and really tried to assist me. They listened to my needs and goals before helping me choose a career field. Although I thought the application process would be quick, it actually took several months. Once I was selected, I had to wait for a slot at Recruiting School to open. In October 1987, I left Mel and our 4-year-old son, Rob, at her parents' home while I headed to Lackland AFB, TX for the seven-week course.

I understood there would be a great deal of study and work involved but was surprised at how compacted everything about the course was designed to be. It was quickly evident that if you were not able to be a bit of a detective, it would be a difficult field to be successful in for any length of time. The written exams were not that difficult, but the mock interviews were anything but straight-forward. They were timed exercises where students talked with one of the instructors pretending they wanted to join the Reserve. While asking these questions, they would throw curveballs with their answers, and each of us were expected to address the issue and guide the conversation. If we missed potential issues that might preclude the individual from joining, forgot the basic script, or did not complete the interview in the allotted time, we failed. I was fortunate in that I did not fail any of these. In fact, I enjoyed them because you had to think on your feet. It was serious, but I made it into a game. Like most things, I found humor in much of it and goofed around quite a bit. Sometimes this did not set well with our instructor, so I had to pull it back and put on my serious face.

As graduation approached, most of those in the class knew where they would be assigned, but I had not heard anything. This troubled me on some levels, but I knew they would figure it out. Part of the issue related to the fact that there were units from two different Numbered Air Forces stationed on March AFB. Whereas the Air Force Reserve is divided into three Numbered Air Forces, 4th, 10th, and 14th, there was a question about whether I would be assigned to a unit in the 4th or 10th Air Force.

On the night of our graduation, a Major from 4th Air Force pulled me aside with the greeting, "So, you're the joker." He did not say it with disdain but rather, as a casual observation. I was a little worried until he explained their dilemma with regards to placing me. Originally, they had planned to send me to the unit in Colorado Springs. However, given how serious the senior recruiter was, they felt that would not work well. They considered sending me to a 10th Air Force unit, but they had their full complement of recruiters. That is when they decided I would be assigned to Travis AFB, a unit in 4th Air Force, just north of San Francisco.

When I called and told Melody where we would be, both of us were happy. This allowed us to still be within a day's driving distance to her parents and oldest sister in the San Diego area, as well as a couple hours south of her other sister in Redding. Melody was excited for me as I was going back on active duty, a place I knew, understood, and loved. It was a time when I could move forward and not worry about finances.

Over the next few weeks, we arranged for our things to be picked up and moved by the military, received my orders, updated ID cards, and said good-bye to friends and family. During a going away party, I expressed that I wondered why God allowed the difficulties of the preceding years. One of the individuals there simply stated, "Maybe it was for us to learn from watching how you addressed issues, grew in your faith, and continued moving forward." It was perhaps the first time that I had ever considered that maybe my struggles were not just about me, but for others as well.

Since neither of us had been to Travis AFB, we read all we could and discovered things to do in the area. The actual trip north was uneventful, and our hearts were full of thankfulness and hope. Once on base, we checked into billeting and were assigned temporary family housing. Since it was the week before Christmas, we purchased a Christmas tree and put it up. We did not know this was not permitted, so when we were told it had to be removed, I wanted to know why. I was not thrilled to tell our three-year-old that the Air Force cancelled Christmas. This was a dilemma but one that needed to be resolved quickly. When they explained it was a fire hazard, I decided I would ask one of the officers at the fire station. The base Fire Marshall wrote a nice letter explaining that as long as the tree was watered, it was not a fire hazard. I put this new 'ornament' in a plastic cover and attached it to the tree. We never heard anything further from the billeting office and our first issue at Travis was resolved! I was happy that I did not have to tell our son the Air Force was Scrooge! What I could not know was that there were other things happening in the reserve recruiting unit at Travis that would not be so easily addressed.

My first day as a recruiter was spent being introduced to the different units, having lunch with the other recruiters, and getting settled into my cubicle. One of the funniest things I saw that day was a grown man, stripped to gym shorts, standing on the scales. I did not know that recruiters were regularly weighed, and this individual was over his maximum weight. He was trying to meet the standard using an unorthodox method. This was not the only unusual activity going on in the unit. In fact, there were several investigations by Headquarters, 4th Air Force, into recruiting improprieties as well as how the recruiting unit was being managed.

After about a month, I was asked to go to McClellan AFB, in Sacramento, to meet the commander and support staff for 4th Air Force Recruiting. While there, I was surprised when the top NCO, a Chief Master Sergeant (referred to as 'Chief'), asked me to let him know if I noticed anything unusual in the office but I was not sure what that meant. It was confusing and I also felt that I was once again being asked by someone in authority to be a snitch. This troubled me on many levels so when I arrived back at the office I talked with my boss about the conversation. I did not know the Chief at 4th Air Force but had found my boss to be straight with me and had already developed some loyalty to him. Apparently, he made it known to 4th that this was unacceptable, and I never heard another word from them about needing information. This lowered my tension and allowed me to focus on my own work.

In January of 1988 we were told Melody was pregnant with our second child, Andy and he was supposed to arrive at the beginning of August. We were both excited, but Melody's morning sickness lasted all day, every day, throughout the entire pregnancy. Within a few short months I was excelling in my role and received many accolades locally as well as at the national level. My success was noticed and with each new plaque, I pushed myself even harder. One of the things that helped was my willingness to work with other recruiters. Sometimes, I would actually connect an individual with a recruiter in another branch, active, reserve or guard, because we did not have what the applicant sought. This meant I had to find someone else to help make my goal, but it was the right thing to do. However, these relationships with recruiters in other services, also garnered good-will towards me as they also referred people to me. It was a win-win situation as I sought to do what was best for each individual. Reserve recruiters need to know the available positions and people in each unit, most successful recruiters spent a great deal of time developing relationships not only with external entities, but also with the leadership in each of the individual units.

Of all the people I met during my time at Travis, Sue Crosby was the one I came to know the best as we were office partners and we both were fairly new to recruiting. She had a sense of humor, an extremely strong work ethic, took her role seriously, and was not above doing anything that needed to be done. If either of us struggled working with an applicant, we would bounce ideas off each other to find the best course of action. Whereas some females preferred talking with a recruiter of the same gender, I was happy to point them in her direction. Although we both were competitive, our goal remained to do what was right and not compromise our integrity.

My career and spiritual life were going well and both Mel and I were connecting to our church. Although I had limited experience with youth groups and was not too thrilled about what I had seen in some youth programs, I was drawn into this ministry by a young, vibrant, and charismatic youth pastor, Mike Brons. When the church began interviewing candidates for the full-time youth position, they narrowed the field down to two individuals. Our introduction to Mike came during a Sunday evening question and answer session. We arrived early as it seemed like many people had expressed interest in attending. As I looked around, I noticed only one person, in the group of about one hundred, who seemed like he might be the candidate. To say I was underwhelmed is putting it mildly. His blond hair was longer than I pictured it should be, he wore a basic shirt with jeans, and had sandals on his feet. I remember thinking, "*Oh, this ought to be good.*" However, as he spoke, there was a maturity and sense of purpose that erased many of my misperceptions. Each time Mike answered a question, I could sense that others were also noticing that he was different than what one might expect from a young youth leader. Before concluding the session, Mike asked, "What do you want from a youth minister and ministry?" As people gave input, he nodded, gracefully commented on the statement, and reaffirmed how important each aspect was. What he did next shocked all of us. He stated, "These are all great, but they are not my responsibility. They are yours as the parent. My role is to come alongside and help you in these tasks." This is when I decided I wanted to work with him. I actually wrote him a note sharing that if he were not selected for this position; he should continue in the direction he was going as what he said was powerful and would have a huge impact for the Kingdom. I also said that if he accepted the position, I would love to become part of his team.

Once Mike was selected, I joined the team. He developed a strong core of adult leaders who would work with the youth for the next few years. Despite being younger than all of us, he was bold in his faith and challenged the youth and adult leaders to live wholeheartedly for Christ. In him I found a kindred spirit and we talked about every aspect of our lives together. One of our conversations involved my not liking "rockier" music. More than anything, it just seemed too loud. However, Mike asked if I had listened to the words. I had not but said I would do that just to see what they were advocating. This was my first introduction to Petra, a group whose songs have come to mean so much in my own journey of faith. Some of you might think they are definitely not a wild group, but at the time, and especially for me, they were way out there!

Mike wanted faith to be real and modeled this in his own life. At the time, Neil Anderson's *The Bondage Breaker*, was all the rage. Given my background, the intensity of my anger, and bitterness from my childhood experiences, I was curious. Some of the book resonated with me so I asked Mike if he would help me look at my life as it related to oppression. Over the course of three evenings Mike and another Christian friend walked me through prayers and helped me address some of these issues. Returning home after our final session I was totally exhausted but was also feeling freer than ever on many levels. I talked with Melody about the discussions, prayers, and how I felt. I also asked her not to share about any of this with anyone else until at least six months had passed. I was concerned that it might be nothing more than an emotional high, similar to what some have after going on a retreat and wanted to reign in any thought to use this as anything that might be construed as a self-seeking moment.

Within a couple months another young couple, Terry, and Rebecca Wraggs, began asking questions because they noticed that a lot of the intensity was gone from my life and words. All I told them was that it was something I needed to watch for a few more months. Unknown to us at the time, they were serious about knowing more and patiently waited. Shortly after the six months was past, they took us out to lunch because they wanted to know what happened. In many ways, I feel like Christ healed a portion of my heart through those prayer sessions. Although I do not believe the enemy can possess one who has chosen to follow Christ, my experience has shown me that there are areas that need to be confessed and turned over to the Lord for healing to take place. Had this experience not brought me closer to the Lord, I might have thought it was an interesting academic exercise. However, the change has held to this day, more than 30 years later.

When I reflect on our time at Travis, it is clear the Lord provided what we needed. Prior to my return to active duty, worries about making a living consumed me. However, having a steady income allowed me to grow in my faith because our basic needs were met. Everyone does not have these same opportunities, and I have often felt guilty about this. I have cried out many times, asking God, "Why me?" Sometimes these words have been from a place of great humility because of all the things our family has enjoyed. He has accomplished His plans for me through specific trials designed for me. My commitment to Him continued growing while stationed in California but there have been many experiences I would rather not have gone through. I was about to discover that some valleys were so deep, so dark, and so lonely, that there would be little encouragement or hope.

Chapter 12
The Deep Pain of Grief

Throughout the four years I was stationed at Travis, I continued my attempts to establish a relationship with my family of origin. We made several trips north to visit my grandfather, aunt, uncle, and cousin in Portland as well as traveling to visit my parents and younger brother, Mike. The trip that brought me the most joy occurred in the early summer of 1989. Jim brought his wife and four children to Seattle, and we spent almost a week with them. It was the first time our families had been together, so we made the most of it. Our time was spent at the Space Needle and Science Center in Seattle, going to Portland, and visiting the pier at Redondo near where we grew up. Our wives were surprised at the energy we showed as Jim and I told stories they had never heard. It was nothing short of delightful as we laughed and cried together. Our bond that had been strong, only grew during that week.

Unfortunately, our parents were upset that they were not the center of attention and let their displeasure be known. Their outbursts might have ruined things had we not kept reminding each other, "Who cares what they think? We are here for each other and if they want to join in, they can."

None of us understood why they still could not connect with us and were not excited to see their children or grandchildren together, happy, and enjoying themselves.

When it was time to go our own ways, my heart was full and for the first time, the tears we shed came from the wonder and amazement of having had such a great time together. I returned to work with a grateful heart. I could only thank the Lord for His work that allowed Jim and I to be connected and nothing was going to interfere with that relationship.

Connecting with people who live across the country was not as easy, or inexpensive, as it is today. If someone were away from their residence, you would leave a message or call back later. Jim called as he often as he could, but it was difficult given that he was driving trucks across the country, and we did not have cell phones at the time. Sometimes, he would call *collect*, which meant I would cover the charges. It did not matter though as it allowed us to talk to one another. Although both Jim and I struggled with depression, the calls after our trip seemed to be more upbeat, filled with laughter, and reaffirmed our love and concern for each other. It was something I never got tired of doing. For me, we were still sharing our lives just as we had on the log so many years before. This brought me great comfort and helped our bond grow.

For many years I had talked about taking Mel and the boys out to see Jim and his family in Ohio. However, we never made the trip as flying was expensive and driving was out of the question due to the distance. It did not bother me to consider the expense as I was generally careful with money, even though Mel is much more pragmatic and frugal by nature. Our vacations were generally spent with her family in Escondido or Redding, or with friends we had established both from Multnomah as well as the Air Force. Life seemed to be moving in a positive direction as we were sound financially, growing spiritually, and I continued doing exceedingly well in my career. In fact, I had found a real niche in some specialized recruiting arenas and had been promoted and received numerous accolades. But I had no idea that a huge emotional tsunami was about to hit and devastate my heart and life.

In May of 1990, Jim called more often, and it was clear that he was struggling with depression and larger questions about life. Although this concerned me, I was not alarmed as we both had our bouts with these darker days. When he called on the evening of June 12th, things were different. He was clearly desperate, broken, and needed to talk. Several times he asked if I, "thought dad loved (him)." Despite my reassurances of my love and that it did not matter if dad loved him or not, he was stuck on that question We talked for several hours and given that it was about 7 p.m. on the west coast when our conversation began, it was already late there. As we talked, something changed in his tone during the fourth hour of conversation. He had moved from questions to reminiscing about our visit the previous year and how he wanted to send a couple things to me. As we ended the conversation, I told him to call me if he needed to talk and I would be there for him. He assured me this would happen and I went to bed satisfied that my words had calmed him.

Like every weekday, I went to work the next morning with little thought about the previous night's conversation as I was more concerned about the high temperature in northern California. It was an important date as *Les Miserables* opened at the Jubilee Center in Calgary and a Boeing 767 would set the record for the longest commercial flight, from Seattle to Nairobi. Continuing my routine, I worked out at the gym after work before riding my bike back to our house on base to enjoy dinner with Mel and the boys. We had just taken our seats when the phone rang. I excused myself and went to the kitchen to answer the phone. On the other end of the line my brother's wife, Diane, sobbed, "John, Jim is gone." Based on the previous evening's conversation, I thought she meant he had left her, and I tried to console her figuring he would come back and call me later. It took a few moments of trying to understand her words through her deep sobs, but I finally realized she meant he had taken his own life.

Now it was my turn to scream. "No! No! No!" I yelled as I threw the phone at the wall, slid to the floor, held my head in my hands, and sobbed like never before. I could not believe that my brother, protector, friend, and confidant was gone. Everything froze and I felt weaker than I had ever been. This was not a dream. No, it was a living nightmare, and I felt sickened to my stomach and cried in agony. At some point, Melody picked up the phone and assured Diane I would catch the first flight I could take. After about an hour I called Diane back and told her I would tell my parents as she had enough to do right then.

Making flight arrangements was not as easy as it is today, and we had to call several airlines before finding one that could get me out that evening. The expense was not even a consideration as I would be there no matter what. Melody arranged for a good friend, Captain Jim Misco, to take us to the San Francisco airport that night while I contacted my supervisor to arrange for emergency leave. Although I tried to contact my parents several times before heading to the airport, there was no answer. Once at the airport, Jim Misco went with us through the whole process and, at some point, explained to a ticketing agent what had happened. During our wait for my flight to depart I was finally able to get ahold of my parents. When I told them that Jim was dead, they explained that the timing was bad as they were going to Reno. I could not believe what I heard and asked for clarification. One might have thought they were in shock had this not been their pattern of life. Having clarified that I heard correctly, my sadness was replaced by a much stronger emotion, anger. I told them that if they did not come to the funeral, and at least respect Jim in death, they would never see my family or me again. Even then, they hesitated to commit as they were concerned about losing their money for the travel package they had bought. As I boarded my flight, I still was not sure whether they would be there or not.

Once on the plane, it was clear to those around me that something major was affecting me, and several people asked if I was OK. Once in the air, a flight attendant came and told me that they were moving me to first class because Jim Misco's conversation with the ticketing agent had been passed along. I was more than a little grateful as my thoughts were so convoluted that it was difficult to focus on much of anything. I wondered why Jim did not call me. I wondered how I missed the obvious signs since I knew those who are suicidal often become calm and try to give things away. Why was God allowing this? Did He just want to see me tortured? I also felt tremendous guilt about not going out to spend time with his family because of financial considerations yet I was flying on an expensive, last minute fare, and my brother was dead. I cried almost the entire way from San Francisco to Detroit, and then from Detroit to Toledo. Despite having been up for more than 24 hours, I could not sleep even after my arrival.

Diane's brother, Dave, greeted me at the airport and although we had never met before, he embraced me and we wept together. Arriving at Jim's home was almost too much to bear. Diane and I could do nothing but sob in each other's arms and begin the difficult journey of grieving the loss of one we loved. There were so many things that needed to be done. I felt it was important to be strong for her and the kids, so I helped plan the day. Our first stop was at the Oregon, OH Police Department since he had killed himself in their jurisdiction. Upon our arrival, we were ushered back to the detective's office. He was a large man with a soft, comforting voice and gentle eyes that looked like he had these conversations too many times. Yet, he did not seem cold or jaded, in fact he was gracious, kind, and almost fatherly in his approach. There were personal belongings to be returned and some questions to help complete their paperwork.

Both Diane and I wanted – needed - to know more about what happened. How, exactly, did he die? Was he alive when they found him? Was there anything else they could tell us about his suicide? The detective asked several questions to make sure we really wanted to know the details as his experience was that this sometimes created more issues for family members. Once we assured him this was important to us, he explained everything from their initial call through the discovery of his body. Apparently, Jim had taken a bunch of sleeping pills, drank several beers, and left the car running in a garage at the house he was watching for a friend. He had written several notes and one was addressed to me. Perhaps the saddest part was that they found his body with his hand latched onto the knob of the door leading back inside the house. It seemed that he had second thoughts and tried to undo what he had started but given everything that was in place, he passed quickly in the darkness, alone.

We left his office with heavier hearts but did not open the letters Jim had left because we still needed to remain somewhat composed since we had to make funeral arrangements. I do not know what I expected at a funeral home but the gentleman at this particular home seemed to enjoy talking about how spending more money would honor Jim's life. I was in no mood for this and told him to quit those tactics. I honestly thought about pummeling him not just for his uncaring attitude but also to vent years of anger over Jim being abused and discarded by others. I wanted to release some of my sadness and grief even as I sought to maintain a sense of decorum. It seemed that even in death, some people wanted to use him for gain. After turning down all the "upgrades," we returned to the house for some rest. However, sleep would not come, especially after reading, and rereading, Jim's note to me. Instead, I tried to comfort the family and help Diane explain to the girls that their dad had gone to sleep. I ate little over the next few days but kept going by consuming copious amounts of Pepsi products.

On the second day in Ohio, Dave drove me to the airport to pick up my parents who had decided to come after all. My dad was totally silent, which was actually all right by me as I was barely keeping years of bitterness and anger under control. However, once they were in the car my mom began berating Jim, talking about how he never amounted to anything, and had cost them a lot of money because of their canceled trip to Reno. As she continued her rant it became more than I could handle. I asked Dave to pull over and made it clear that she could either show Jim the respect he deserved in life, and never received, or we would take them back to the airport right then. I believe my tone, intensity, and facial expression made things clear. Years of just letting her talk bad about him had reached the breaking point. Although she did not talk openly during the next three days, she pouted and tried to bring the focus of attention on her as opposed to Diane and the kids. It was true that Jim had struggled with many things in life, but all of us kids did. Given the home life we had, who wouldn't have struggled with mental health and addiction issues? What her and dad never seemed to cherish was the fact that Jim had been clean for several years, was holding down a job, and seemed to be doing better in life. For me, these things mattered more than his past battles. His victories more than covered for any past struggles. To Diane and me, he was valuable and loved.

I stayed several days after the funeral but needed to return to work. It was only after the service that my body totally collapsed, and I was able to sleep. Even then, the sleep was interrupted by nightmares of Jim calling me to open the door and let him out. Numerous times I woke up shaking, screaming, and crying as I relived what I thought were his final moments. My faith in God was there, but I wrestled with why a loving God allowed this to happen. I shouted accusations into the sky while sitting at Jim's grave. It seemed that I was back in my youth, walking to school, calling out for relief. And, like before, it did not come. Instead, my mind reflected on a conversation that I observed in a theology class during my senior year at Multnomah.

Like me, one of my professors at Multnomah, Dr. Al Baylis, had suffered the loss of someone he loved. Since we attended the same church with his family, we interacted with them every week. On Palm Sunday 1985, his wife was killed in a tragic accident but he only took a couple weeks off before returning to the classroom. As students, none of us could believe he was back so soon. There was an underlying tension during his first few days in the class until a student finally interrupted his lecture to ask the question many of us had: "How can you be here right now?" Many were visibly shocked at such a bold, and seemingly cold, question but Al seemed unphased by it. His simple response was, "I know the character of my God." This was not a judgment on the student who had the audacity to ask; instead, it was the statement of a man who had seen God work in his heart and life. Dr. Baylis spoke the words with an air of confidence that deeply moved me. It also caused me to ask questions about how I viewed the Lord. What did I really know about His character? Did I live according to those truths, or did I just give lip service? The previous chapters make the answer to this question clear. I believe you know my answer, and it is not flattering. I really had not considered this important aspect of my faith. However, sitting by my brother's grave, God challenged me not just about my attitude over His right to direct things, but also my arrogance in the demands I made, and expectations I had, about Him.

I knew from Ephesians that God is motivated by love and I am the beneficiary of His work. This has come through physical provisions of money and food when we were in need, as well as gentle conviction, encouragement, and restoration as I spent time considering the Scriptures and their implications for my life. He always seemed to bring things to mind as I read the Bible and was forced to look into my heart.

I often recall an assignment Dr. Sauerwein gave us while studying Colossians 3. As I worked on the assignment, I had a choice to make. I could just write something that was more of an overview, or I could share about how the Lord had convicted me that what Paul calls us to in verses 12–17 did not characterize my life. With a broken heart, I chose to share about the latter. Why? Simply put, this passage impacted me so directly that I had no other choice. It was like the Lord had shined an intense light on the darkness within my own heart. In His love, He convicted me so that I might become more like Him.

Although I had been growing in those areas after college, I struggled with how Jim's death reflected this love. I could not know it at the time, but having the knowledge of, and trust in, the reality that God loved me, and continued working with me, would sustain me in the coming days when depression, despair, anger, and bitterness sought to overtake my heart and life.

Chapter 13
The Larger Kingdom

Once I returned home, I found little satisfaction in much of anything. Despite being the number two recruiter in the nation, my ever-present depression overwhelmed me. The place where I found real solace, and felt I had friends, was at church. On many occasions Mike Brons would listen and comfort me in a manner that has helped me know how to care for and comfort others. It never ceased to amaze me how much he gently challenged some misconceptions I had about faith, God, life, and caring for others.

The following Christmas, our family flew out to Diane's and spent it with her family. While it was an enjoyable time together, there was the awkward reality that Jim was absent. By this time, Diane had begun the work of moving on and was seeing another gentleman, Rick, who we instantly liked. He seemed serious on many levels, but I was impressed with how he treated Diane as well as his sense of humor. By the time we left, I was happy to see that she was finding love again, despite the sadness of Jim's suicide.

Although I could not know it at the time, our family would begin a series of moves over the next six years that would be extremely important in my own faith journey. However, one of the most amazing things happened during those final months at Travis. As we remained in contact with Diane and Rick, they not only got married but also made the decision to begin attending church on a regular basis and follow Christ. I marveled at how God was working. In short order, they made changes that often take others, including me, years, or even decades, to accomplish. I could only attribute it to God's convicting work and faithfulness.

Jim's children have walked through their own valleys wrestling with their father's death, but I knew that these battles were beyond my ability to address. While I wanted an answer from God about what good Jim's death had accomplished, it was difficult not to see this transformation as being part of His work. I had to confess my attitude and arrogance because it was clear that He continued working in people's hearts. This did not mean I was at peace with Jim's suicide, but my heart moved a few more degrees towards full acceptance that God's character is loving and compassionate.

In 1992, I was selected for a recruiting position in Pocatello, ID, about two and a half hours north of Salt Lake City where Hill AFB is located. At the time, it had just a little over 46,000 people so it was a very different culture from what we were used to.

This was a rural community where most of the people in the area hunted and more than 75% would identify themselves as being members of the Church of Jesus Christ, Latter Day Saints (LDS or Mormon). We were able to move into a comfortable home in Chubbuck and found a church community we would call home, I continued coaching soccer, and both Mel and I grew in our faith and served others. But it was not attending church that stimulated our spiritual journeys the most. Instead, it was a very eclectic group of people from different countries and states who began meeting together to discuss larger issues of life.

Although my role at Travis AFB seldom required me to travel overnight, I began traveling at least once a month west to Mountain Home AFB, near Boise, north to Malmstrom AFB, outside of Great Falls, MT, and south to Hill AFB near Salt Lake City. Given the scarcity of radio stations in many of these areas, a cell phone with *Pandora* would have been a huge help on the long drives! However, since these things were not available, I spent hundreds of hours listening to the Bible on CD. This allowed me to discover things I had missed before and found that I could concentrate more since I was not just skimming through the different books and had few distractions. This became a pattern that has remained a strong, transformative, routine for almost three decades.

Although I enjoyed these times it was when I returned and talked about what I was learning with the other people in our weekly meetings that I was able to process my thoughts more fully.

One of the couples in this group, Eric and Christina Comparini, were from Sau Paulo, Brazil. He was a computer engineer, she was a pharmacist, and they had a son and daughter close to our boys' ages. Christina and Melody initially met through a water aerobics class while Eric and I began our own conversations when we arrived to pick our wives up. Both Eric and Christina were growing in their faith, and we developed our friendship while sharing meals and visiting at each other's homes after church, as well as getting together several times throughout the week. They introduced us to other Brazilians in the area as well as a couple from Iran. When I first met the Iranian couple, my prejudice against them was barely under the surface. Despite the years since the Iranian hostage crisis, I was still angry at anything Iranian. However, as we got to know them through conversations and picture books about Iran, I had to confess my unwarranted prejudicial attitude towards an entire people group. I came to enjoy this couple, their food, and their openness to not only interact with Americans, but also to listen to the message of Christ and His work. We spent many evening just talking about cultural things and enjoying ethnic foods. They helped me realize that prejudices come from places of ignorance, darkness and are often coupled with an unwillingness to look inward at the real issue.

While there were several international people in this blossoming group, we also had a couple from a Mennonite background, an Army recruiter, and his family, as well as another couple who had been on the mission field. We studied the Bible and had open question and answer sessions about what it meant to follow Christ and interact with the world around us. At some point we decided that a focused study might be helpful, so we spent months watching Francis Schaeffer's, *How Should We Then Live?* I had heard about these films while at the Christian Servicemen's Center in Germany, but after watching the first two films back then, I had absolutely no idea what he was talking about. However, this time it was different because I had a larger understanding of the Bible and additional life experiences. Despite there being between six and ten young children present during our weekly get togethers, we did not have child-care. Instead, we let them play quietly in the same room where we watched these films and had our discussions. We normally talked late into the evening hours and children were often found in various parts of the house either sleeping, playing, or reading when we finally ended our evening.

We were discovering a wider meaning to the term *Christian Community*. It was like we were all part of a larger family that saw religious discussions as a normal part of our interactions. Often, we would head to Yellowstone or other places as a group. We loved one another and celebrated each other's unique gifts. Over the last three decades we have lost contact with most of these people, but our friendship with the Comparinis remains strong to this day and it has been enjoyable to see the families of our oldest son and their daughter become friends as adults who are parenting their own children.

Like the Hospitality House, community was the central core of our relationships. This did not mean we were always wonderful or understanding. However, we were honest and expressed concerns in a loving manner. We sought to encourage each other in our individual walks with God so that we could serve those around us. These people had become our family, and, unlike my family of origin, we sought to resolve any differences in an amiable manner because of our shared love of the Lord and one another.

While stationed in Pocatello, we continued to reach out to my family in Washington and Oregon. At one point we invited my parents to come for a visit. As always, it was tense, but we wanted to find a way to connect with them. Unlike Reno, and other tourist destination cities, there was not a lot to do where we lived except enjoying the outdoors, natural hot springs, or visiting with others. When they came to our house, I took some time off so we could drive to Yellowstone as I thought it might be a good opportunity to enjoy a favorite activity of ours. If one has not experienced the beauty of the various eco-systems in this National Park it is difficult to describe. Like Yosemite, it is a place of wonderous marvels that sometimes defy the imagination. The topography, animals, flora, fauna, and wandering rivers make it a great place to slow down and really enjoy all that is around us. However, the trip was another failed attempt to find common ground. When they headed back home my heart was heavy, wondering if we would ever find a way to relate to them on any level.

In the summer of the same year, my aunt Sharon, Uncle Tom, and their son Drew, came and spent several days with us in Yellowstone. Our time was filled with laughter, fishing in the streams, seeing the sights, drinking lots of bottled Pepsi, and Uncle Tom teaching us how to play cribbage. It was everything I had hoped would happen with my mom and dad but did not. Like the times I spent with my aunt and her family while I was growing up, the time together enjoying Yellowstone strengthened our bonds. Before leaving, Tom bought me a cribbage board from the gift shop that we still use today! Every time we play cribbage, which is frequently, I think back on those days with great fondness. My relationship with them was, and remains, what I believe a family should be. We do not always agree with each other on every issue but there remains a respect, appreciation, and a commitment to one another similar to what we found with our group of friends in Idaho. What I could not have known at the time was that cancer was destroying Uncle Tom's lungs and this would be the last time I would see him.

As we prepared to leave Idaho in February 1994, we spent the last week with Eric and Christina as our belongings had once again been packed, loaded, and were on their way to our next assignment in Georgia. The thought of leaving was difficult as we had become so close with them, and all of us struggled to keep our emotions under control. During dinner, the night before we left, I stated that I still did not know why we had been brought to Pocatello, ID – a place we literally had to locate on a map when I was given orders to move. With tears in her eyes, Christina said, "John, God brought you here for us."

It was one of those moments when I missed the obvious because my focus remained on me as opposed to others. I remembered my conversation with friends several years before as we left Escondido and headed to Travis AFB. God had taken us to another location for two years, to mold and encourage others in their lives and faith journeys. The point was becoming clearer, God will move and use us in unexpected ways.

Early the next morning, during a serious snowstorm, we left in our two vehicles for my next duty assignment in Warner Robins, Georgia. In ten hours of travel, we were only able to cover about 120 miles as the roads were getting worse due to snow, ice, and strong winds. We pressed on because we were in the middle of Wyoming and there were no towns to stop in. Finally, we stopped for the night in a town because the roads were closed due to the weather. Mel and I were exhausted and wanted nothing more than dinner and sleep. However, two young boys needed to run around as they had been sitting in the cars for so long. So, the long day extended into the evening and sleep would remain elusive.

Before leaving Pocatello, I told my aunt I would check in with her each day since Uncle Tom was in the latter stages of his battle with cancer. I called Sharon that night and she told me Tom had passed away. This news broke my heart, and, despite the snow, I went outside wearing flip flops, shorts, and a jacket. Once again, I looked towards the heavens and cried tears of deep sorrow. Uncle Tom seemed to be larger than life. He always had a bottle of Pepsi and an unfiltered Camel cigarette in his hand, and it was the latter that took his life. He made me laugh and seemed to have a ready smile that went well with his teasing. He showed us boys how to make a silencer for a pistol using bottle caps from Pepsi bottles, and introduced me to the outdoors, fishing, and camping. Aunt Sharon and Uncle Tom took me to Jantzen Beach where I had my first corn dog, and that trip is still one of my favorite childhood memories. He helped me endure so many years of abuse and laid important groundwork for who I would become today, but now he was gone. I was unable to attend the funeral because the military grants only so many days between leaving one duty station and arriving at the next. Even as I write this, the tears are flowing freely as I recall the many wonderful moments I had with him.

During the rest of our trip to Georgia, I alternated between weeping about the loss and laughing at funny experiences we had together. As we went further south, the snow and ice disappeared, and the warmth of the sun became our companion. We also noticed the people spoke a different language that sounded like English but seemed to have extra syllables; it was Southern. If you have not spent time in the southern states, this probably sounds far-fetched, but we had a difficult time understanding some of the people we encountered at restaurants, service stations, and hotels. We soon learned to just nod and move along. In many ways, it was more difficult than the move to Germany because I did not expect things to be so different in the United States but did when I went to Germany.

Upon our arrival at Robins AFB, Georgia, a little over 100 miles south of Atlanta, we set about getting an apartment and checking in for my new assignment at Headquarters, Air Force Reserve Recruiting. My new role required traveling to various locations around the US to perform both inspection and training at each Reserve unit, managing waivers for individuals seeking to join the Air Force Reserve, advocating for improvements in our processes at headquarters, helping recruiters when they encountered issues they could not resolve, and doing general staff work for both the actual Air Force Reserve headquarters as well as reports for the Pentagon. Although it was demanding, it was a place where my skillsets blossomed and were recognized by all levels of the Air Force Reserve Command.

I found that when I worked hard, others noticed and were willing to mentor me. Although I worked with many great people while in Georgia, Lt. Col. Mickelson helped me grow in my career as well as set me up for success even after leaving the Air Force.

He was methodical, quiet, and looked like a distinguished southern officer. He had a background with public affairs and journalism and therefore, had little patience for poor writing. He was the one who signed anything leaving the building, so we interacted on a daily basis. Most of my correspondence during the first few months was returned, looking like he had sliced his hand while reading them because there were so many red marks on them. At first, my attitude was less than pleasant about his corrections. However, I also realized this was an opportunity to develop my writing skills and began to ask questions about why the corrections were needed. By the time I headed to my next assignment, he had developed enough confidence in my writing that he signed the letters without much review. This reassured me that I had learned a great deal from him.

Like so many things in rural Georgia, church was different. I was surprised that people usually wore suits, or at least shirts and ties, to church and most attended services twice on Sunday and again on Wednesday night. Having gone to churches that were either non-denominational, or autonomous from governing bodies, I did not know how to begin working within the framework of an organization that provided direct oversight for individual churches. During our time in Warner Robins, we attended Southern Baptist, North American Baptist, and a Christian Missionary Alliance churches at various times. Although we met many believers who really sought to follow, love, and serve the Lord, we also found a reluctance by several pastors, and leaders, to consider some of their practices in light of Scripture. This resulted in some awkward conversations that have greatly impacted my own views on church, leadership in church bodies, and funding building projects. Although we talked with church leadership several times, there were two conversations that stood out.

The first occurred shortly after we began attending a small church. We were drawn to this particular body because of the warmth of several people we first met. Although the preaching was usually topical, we were open to new approaches and felt they were orthodox in their views on scripture. Our boys attended a weekly program called *A Workman and Not Ashamed*, or AWANA that helped teach, and reinforce Biblical principles. They also played games and competed in what is known as circle games. While the boys were at AWANA, I attended the prayer time in the sanctuary and Melody remained home and worked on homeschool lesson plans. On one of those evenings, the pastor and his 15-year-old son asked questions about whether Melody was a believer. Although some had questioned my faith in the past, this was new territory for me as Melody has always held tenaciously to her faith since a young age. When I asked what led them to believe my wife might not be a Christian, without hesitation they responded, "Well, she continually wears pants to church and does not attend the prayer meetings." I was incredulous and actually began laughing. This only infuriated them, and they immediately ended our conversation. What was especially sad is that the son did most of the talking while his father seemed to encourage this self-righteous attitude. Although the boys continued in AWANA through the rest of the program year, we began looking for another church.

It was at this second church where we encountered some similar issues, but on a much grander scale. This church had a large, ornate, building and several hundred regularly attended every Sunday. Like the church we had just left, the pastor focused on topical issues but was much more intense and confident than the previous pastor. We began to get involved and I facilitated an adult Sunday School class. However, the pastor and several of the deacons expressed concern because I did not use the approved curriculum. After a few visits to the class, they seemed to accept what was happening because

I was only using the Bible, was prepared with questions, and encouraged discussion. After a few months the pastor expressed his frustration at how many people were attending and felt I was trying to "steal them away." This was definitely not my intent but led to him publicly questioning both Mel and me both in conversations and from the pulpit.

Despite this, God used this class to encourage people to reach others in the community. When leading studies, I am more of a facilitator as opposed to one who lectures. I appreciated difficult questions and not having pat answers. We watched this group move from just reading the Bible and praying for others to actually reaching out to those who needed help. I was proud of them for moving out of their comfort zone and serve those outside the church.

While living in Georgia, *Promise Keepers* was a thriving organization that held men's conferences around the country. Thousands attended these events as the messages were encouraging, challenging, and dealt with principles for Christian living as well as social issues. That year, the focus was on how segregated churches were. Different ethnicities not worshipping together made no sense to me as the military does a good job of weeding out those who cannot interact, work, and/or live with individuals from all ethnicities and walks of life. The idea of churches being isolated, homogeneous, bodies was something that troubled Mel and me from our earliest days in Georgia.

Many men from the church attended the Atlanta *Promise Keepers* conference. Most of us left it with hopes that this would be the start of something new in our church as well as in the larger body of Christ in the Warner Robins area. However, with nothing more being said about the issue after several months, Mel and I met with the pastor. We wanted to know when we might connect with an African American church that was literally across the highway from where our church was located. Neither of us were prepared for his response. There was an uncomfortable pause before he leaned back in his stout office chair, cupped his hands behind his head, and said, "We are just not ready for that yet." Melody immediately asked when they might be ready, and I sarcastically added, "It has only been like 150 years!" We left there with heavy hearts, and I could barely contain my anger at the whole situation.

Despite living in Europe and doing temporary assignments in the Far East, as well as in several states, we had never seen or experienced, overt racism on the scale that we witnessed in rural Georgia. Yes, there were prejudicial things happening on both sides, but seldom did anyone speak up. One of the bumper stickers we often saw on cars summed up a common sentiment, "We Don't Care How You Do it in the North!" Our experiences there propelled me to recognize that there were serious racial divisions in our country, helped me realize that I needed to speak up for individuals who were experiencing discriminatory practices, and drove me to work to bring unity within the communities where we lived.

Although we had concerns with the attitude of the lead pastor, the Lord provided several strong southern, Christian, families who became dear friends. We spent many weekends with the Taylors and Jenkins who really sought to live for Christ. They helped us appreciate the good parts of being southerners and kept our hearts from becoming prejudiced about the south by what we saw as problems within the church in Georgia. Their graciousness and willingness to allow us to be part of their larger families gave us a sense of connection similar to what we experienced in Idaho.

While stationed in Georgia, my dad passed away. I went on emergency leave to help my mom with all the things that need to be accomplished when someone dies. At the time, we did not have the money for Melody or the boys to join me. However, a dentist from the church bought Melody a ticket, and three families watched the boys for a full week without our asking. They had become our family, not just in the Lord, but also in the fullest sense of being part of their group. Once again, the compassion of others touched me deeply and allowed me to see sacrificial love in action. Although we would leave this church, we have remained in touch with two of the families for over thirty years.

As we began looking for another place to worship, we discovered a Christian Missionary Alliance church and were pleasantly surprised by what we found. While they were not a large body of believers and had an unimpressive building and a pastor who was not dynamic, they were serious about their faith and opened their hearts and arms to everyone. I cannot tell you about a specific message that changed my life. I do not recall particular conversations when I had an "aha" moment. However, I can speak about the hospitality, love, grace, and gentleness of many individuals and families.

One of the families, the Castellanos, were living examples of individuals who practiced their faith. The husband was a landscaper from Belgium, while the mother came from a traumatic life that, in many ways, made mine seem docile. They understood brokenness, living in a broken world, were not wealthy by any human standard but lived honest, contented, lives. Their love for the Lord and heart attitudes helped me grow in my faith more than hundreds of sermons I have heard over the last four decades. Once again, God used others to model what it looked like to really seek after Him, become more conformed to His image, and how to love others.

I have always appreciated how Christ interacted with those who came to Him, no matter what their cultural heritage or religious beliefs were. We were the benefactors experiencing the same attitude of love and compassion from so many others in each of our assignments while in the military. Despite differences in culture, and experiences, fellow believers sought to love us as their own family because of the work Christ had done in their hearts.

Spending time with these friends gave insight into their hearts and helped us to see them as individuals made in God's image. When one encounters people who hold different views, practice their faith differently, or are caught in the darkness of the enemy's traps, it is difficult to not be moved. It has been through these encounters, and many other experiences, that Christ has developed and refined my heart so that I can see people as broken vessels. As such, I cannot just turn away from them. Instead, I am drawn towards them with a heart of compassion and understanding, without rancor or judgment.

Chapter 14
On the Road Again

Our time in Georgia would soon end with new orders to the Air Reserve Personnel Center in Denver, Colorado. We always wanted to live in Colorado, so all of us were eagerly anticipating the change of scenery, the chance to enjoy snow again, as well as the outdoor opportunities available there. This would be a unique assignment as there would only be two of us, a Lieutenant Colonel (LTC) and myself, who would be interacting, and managing the Individual Mobilization Augmentee (IMA) program. This is not a well-known program but has existed since the earliest days when the Air Force became its own branch of service. These positions are not like traditional reservists who serve at least one weekend a month and two weeks a year with their assigned reserve unit. Instead, IMA's are assigned to active-duty Air Force and Joint Service units, and have flexible schedules. Individuals in this program coordinate with their unit of assignment to create a training schedule that meets the needs of both the unit and the individual to support both peacetime and wartime missions. They also often deploy sooner than other reserve forces.

Early in my recruiting career I discovered that this was a great opportunity with lots of flexibility for those needing it. Further, the active-duty units were grateful to have fully qualified individuals assist them. Unlike regular recruiting, and before standard computer programs allowing quick access to copious amounts of information, I was continually on the phone coordinating paperwork, making trades in positions, and maintaining regularly updated lists of the various entities and positions. While some recruiters found it frustrating, I found it enjoyable, and the leadership knew I understood this program and had the connections to help other recruiters as they sought to place applicants in these positions.

During my first few days on the job, I realized that the secretary, Diane, seemed extremely distant and almost cold, towards me. She had been in the federal civil service for nearly thirty years, and I soon discovered that she had really been treated poorly by her current supervisor. As we worked together, she became a new person and offered to help with all manner of projects and had some really good ideas. Unfortunately, the officer assigned to work with us during the first five months was not the most capable and continued treating her with disdain. When I broached the subject with him, I was strongly encouraged to "stay in my own lane." I kept my distance from him and worked through other individuals to get my job done.

When he retired LTC Michael Oswald was assigned as his replacement. Both Diane and I were relieved and excited because I knew him from my time at headquarters and found him to be a real leader. Where the previous colonel was selfish, rude, abrasive and enjoyed ensuring everyone understood he was in charge, LTC Oswald was the opposite. He was soft spoken, humble, sought to find common ground when working in teams, and continually supported those he worked with. Although he had never been married, he often asked about my family and ensured I had time off to tend to their needs and be there for their activities. He was conservative by nature, took piano lessons, and while eccentric in many ways, never seemed to worry about how people viewed him.

While in Georgia, I found that while he was sometimes confused by my humor, he seemed to tolerate my teasing and pranks that came as part of working with me. In my mind, he was, and remains, one of the finest officers I worked with at any time during my military career.

The three of us soon became a team that worked together, respected the roles and strengths of one another, and began the larger task of developing better relationships with each of the IMA program managers. Professionally, it was one of the best assignments I had despite being on the road more than half of the time.

With traveling being such a big part of my career for years it was not too surprising that our marriage was sometimes strained. Unlike my father, I tried to use any opportunity to connect with the boys through activities, regular reading, playing many board games, teaching them about the outdoors, and coaching soccer. Although I was well respected in my military roles and was very focused on being a father who made time for his boys, I had not given as much attention to making or maintaining a healthy marriage. In many ways, I went through the motions, but a chasm was growing between Melody and me. Seldom did I ask about her own concerns as she took care of things while I was traveling, handling everything from mail and bills to car and house maintenance. It became a lonely life for both of us, and we began to live parallel lives. While it was not insurmountable, this was something that would need to be addressed in the coming years.

Although work took a great deal of energy and time, I still enjoyed participating in our church. It was larger than the ones we had previously attended and was located just outside of Aurora, a suburb of Denver. The pastor was dynamic, seemed to live what he spoke, and tried to connect with people throughout the church despite its size. At the time there were two opportunities to work with high school students. One was the more traditional youth program, and the other was the AWANA program designed for teenagers. I opted to work with the latter as our boys were familiar with AWANA. It was a natural connection, and we believed the teaching to be sound. I enjoyed ministering with the other adults and connected with the students. However, I was unprepared for the intensity of the competitiveness between the two youth programs. Good families had strong disagreements over which one should receive the church's support. Further, those of us in the AWANA program tended to be homeschoolers while those in the traditional program generally had students in the public schools. Throughout our time there, the chasm between the groups seemed to only grow.

Like many, I clung to the view that the other group was suspect and even compromising their Christian beliefs. I would like to say my attitude was correct, but in this instance, I was as much a part of the problem as anyone else. This experience once again revealed my own arrogance and called it what it was, sin.

Throughout my life I had sought to be noticed. While it is not wrong to advance in a career, lead studies, or participate in different ministries within a church, it is wrong to make it so what I was doing was more important or more ethical than the work of others. All of us were trying to minister, parent, and live our faith the best we could. That meant I should have reflected the heart of Christ, been supportive of those efforts, and loved the other parents and their students. This revelation hit me hard, and I had to confess it as opposed to excusing it. I also learned that although it is good to help others outside of one's own family, it should never be at their expense. These lessons would become even more ingrained when we went to my next duty assignment as the Senior Recruiter in Portland, Oregon.

Anyone familiar with the political and social dynamics in Portland knows there has long been a schism between the military and various factions in the area. I first came to understand the pressures faced by recruiters there while assigned to headquarters in Georgia. When the Senior Recruiter position in Portland was initially offered to me, I turned it down. However, after a couple days pondering the idea, I felt like it was where we needed to go and accepted the assignment. It was clear the role would be demanding but I had been helping address recruiting issues across the country, so I felt ready to tackle this newest project. I was excited to return to the northwest, which meant I could spend more time with my relatives in Portland and live among long-time friends of ours.

We had not lived in Oregon since 1985 but returned to the church we attended in Sandy, a town about 45 minutes east of Portland. When we left, Fellowship Bible Church (FBC) had over 250 people and was a thriving church with a vibrant outreach. Mel and I appreciated that most took their faith seriously and sought to live in a manner that reflected the love of Christ to a lost community, and the elders were focused on the actual spiritual well-being of the people they served. However, we soon discovered that things had changed. The church was much smaller, several elders had left, and there was tension within the body related to things that had occurred in the intervening 13 years. While the number of people attending a church has never been an issue for us, we were concerned about the divisions we noticed.

Our closest friends of forty years, Paul and Susan Winsinger, helped us put the pieces together about what occurred during our absence. That information helped us understand some of the issues as we reconnected with others at the church.

The work of a Senior Recruiter is seldom slow or dull, and brought together all the skills I developed throughout my recruiting career. The role required excellent communication skills as well as an ability to develop community awareness about the role of the Air Force Reserve and specifically, the mission of the 939th Rescue Wing. I was fortunate that my Wing Commander, Colonel Rusty Moen, and the other officers in the unit, fully supported our efforts. Several of these officers went on to become one, and two, star generals – something that seldom occurs even in much larger units.

In 2000, my grandfather's health was declining, and my aunt had most of the responsibility of caring for him. As his strength waned, I visited him often as it was on my way home from the office. While there, I usually sat on the couch by the front window looking at the kitchen that held so many wonderful memories. I thought about all the pancakes he made for all of us and the many meals he grilled on a charcoal BBQ. I remembered playing and sleeping in the garage, going to a house fire with him and coming home smelling like smoke, and going to church and enjoying the solemn services. I wished my grandmother had not died when I was in junior high and was saddened by the knowledge that he too would soon be gone. He died peacefully one evening while I was there with him. I called my aunt after he passed and then knelt beside his bed and said good-bye.

I poured myself into work to ease the pain of losing my grandfather. It allowed me to stay busy instead of just focusing on the pain I felt. I thanked the Lord as I could see how He had orchestrated my assignment to Portland so that I was able to be there for both my aunt and grandfather. However, it would soon be abundantly clear that I was not appreciative or grateful for His work when my physical body, coupled with my emotional health, began to fail.

One morning while driving to work in Georgia I had moved to the center lane waiting to make the left turn into the parking lot of our off-base office. Everything was going smoothly. As I waited to cross the oncoming lanes of traffic, my car was rear-ended by a pickup that was traveling a little over 50 mph. Apparently, the driver had dropped his cigarette on the floor and inadvertently swerved when he bent down to pick it up. Although I was in some pain, it did not seem too bad at the time. However, within a few hours I discovered that I had extreme whip lash. This would prove to be problematic and remains so today. Within a few months, I found that certain exercises exacerbated the symptoms, and this began limiting my ability to do things.

After about a year in Portland, I began experiencing extreme pain in my lower back that extended down my right leg. After many visits to the emergency room, the doctors discovered herniated discs pressing on nerves as well as the fact that I had ankylosing spondylitis – a very painful, genetic disease. This led to several back surgeries, two while on active duty and three since retiring. These continuous waves of nerve pain throughout my back and leg prevented me from doing most of the things I enjoyed. Hiking in the woods was out. Soccer, deck hockey, and weightlifting were no longer options for exercise. Even running on a treadmill or using a stationary bike became too painful to endure. Standing on concrete became its own torture, and I became less mobile and gained weight.

During the same period, I was also struggling emotionally and spiritually. My role as the senior recruiter was already stressful, but all of the requirements to be on my feet throughout the day began taking a toll. I could not understand why God allowed these things to happen and I became angry. I believed He brought me to Portland and my career would end on a high note. The pain was not part of the picture I envisioned. In fact, I really thought I had it all figured out. However, a great darkness began to descend on me like it had during my early days in elementary school and junior high. I was losing my ability to concentrate as the pain assaulted my body each day. Life was becoming focused on managing pain as opposed to enjoying my final assignment.

Although I was able to retire in March 2003, it was like a marathoner who had nothing left at the finish line. I did not know what to expect as a civilian because I had literally spent more than sixty percent of my life in the military. However, it was time to transition to living life as a civilian and begin a new season of life.

Chapter 15
Brokenness and Despair

In the months leading up to my retirement, I accepted the role as pastor at FBC and decided to attend seminary at the same time. Although I enjoyed mentoring individuals and couples, teaching from the Word, studying the Bible, and coming alongside people in times of crisis, I was not prepared for the behind-the-scenes expectations people have for pastors and their families. Sometimes the nitpicking, rude comments, and outright sabotaging overwhelmed me. The emotional energy required was tremendous. I was blindsided by the intense personal attacks not only by a few members in the body but also those who were serving as elders. I quickly understood more about the behind-the-scene politics that has destroyed many churches.

The role of a pastor is taxing in the best of circumstances, and FBC was anything but this. Much of the encouragement I found came not from the leaders at the church but from a couple of mentors at the seminary. I found that my studies were much easier than working on my undergraduate degree and helped reinforce many of the ideas I tried to implement. In fact, unlike my previous experience at Multnomah, I was the one with a great deal of hands-on experience and Bible knowledge. Most students were in their mid-twenties and had little practical experience, but I was in my mid-forties and had completed a career that took me around the country and world. All the hours listening to Scripture while traveling, coupled with reading and studying it on my own, had generated a renewed heart that was focused on growing and serving. Other students sought me out, and I became a mentor for many of them. Further, I made the commitment to be honest about whether I actually completed my reading assignments or not, willingly submitted to their rules – much easier since they had changed over the years! – and coordinated my messages with my classes to prevent doubling my workload. I soon discovered a kindred spirit in two of my professors, Dr. Paul Metzger and Dr. Blum.

Paul taught theology. He tried to make it practical and asked difficult questions that often made us uncomfortable. At the time, Oregon had a measure on the ballot that would legalize the marriage of same sex couples. In the evangelical world there were strong, and often nasty and sarcastic, comments against this with what was called the "One Man, One Woman" campaign. I struggled not so much with their view but rather, their tone. At meetings with the Sandy ministerial association, each of the pastors was given yard signs to hand out at church. However, I could not bring myself to do it. I was just becoming friends with our neighbor whose son was gay. I felt the sign would be the antithesis of everything I believed about how to love others and come alongside them, wherever they were. My position was not well received by several of the other pastors in the association.

Later, before the election, Paul Metzger organized a panel conversation that brought together several hundred people on both sides of the issue into a large classroom in the library at Multnomah University. The panel laid out the guidelines; homosexuals, bisexuals, and evangelicals all sat mixed together; and over a two-hour period, everyone listened respectfully. Honest questions were politely asked and when it was over almost everyone stayed and talked with one another without concern for which camp they were in. I left with tears of joy because this is how adults, especially Christians, should approach difficult social issues. I do not think many minds were changed, but it was clear that some stereo-types were challenged.

Dr. Metzger was also a huge, active, voice for social justice. Although I did not agree with everything he advocated, his work with John Perkins and people of color was what I hoped would happen after the *Promise Keepers* event in Atlanta many years before. Paul introduced me to an African American pastor, Donald Frazier, who led a church in a rougher neighborhood of Portland. As our friendship grew, we thought it would be good to connect our two churches. Several from our church visited theirs several times and I was given the opportunity to speak at two of their services. My heart was full because this was something I had only dreamed about. In the same vein, Donald came out to share the Word at our church and their choir led us in worship. I had a growing expectation that this would be the beginning of larger things.

However, one of the elders and several in the congregation, were less than enthused by this interaction. One actually told me, "They are sure fun to watch jumping around." Comments like this shocked me to the core. When I broached the subject of allowing our youth to spend a week working at their church and seeing what life was like in their neighborhoods, several dug in their heels and felt it was unsafe but acknowledged that we might be a big help to them. However, I felt they had it backwards. We would be learning from *them*. I found myself questioning why we sent youth thousands of miles away to Europe and Mexico for missions but were reticent about going 30 miles to assist our brothers and sisters. My heart broke and it would be many years before that wound began to heal. I was beginning to realize that there was little I could do to change things since changing hearts is in God's realm, not mine. My role was to shepherd the congregation through my words, actions, and more importantly, by considering what the Bible said about our hearts, God, and what following Christ meant.

There was another professor, Dr. Blum, who helped me in this work. He taught about worship and spiritual disciplines and his assignments made a huge difference in my heart and life. For many years I had struggled with worship because I viewed it as being more than just singing. I believed it should include introspection, confession, and scripture readings as well. Dr. Blum broadened my understanding through practical work in spiritual disciplines like meditating on portions of scripture and the work Christ did for us, as well as fasting, prayer, and reflection.

Much of my life is filled with noise. I love talk radio, music, gatherings of people, and seemed to study best when there was something happening in the background. Our class went on two retreats where we practiced what we had been learning. It was the first time in my life I was able to move away from the noise and distractions to focus on my heart attitude towards God and others. It was a rich time that allowed me to experience silence and solitude and just focus on my communion with the Lord.

At this same time, my medical conditions deteriorated, and I went into deeper depression. Although my spiritual life was changing, I still felt God was not upholding His part by not alleviating my constant pain. To escape, I turned to my drug of choice: gambling. During one of my military trips another recruiter taught me how to play two specific card games as well as the faster paced game of *Craps*. Although my trips to casinos were only occasional while I was in the Air Force, I began to go to a small casino about 45 minutes north of where we lived.

It was not long before I could not get enough of the euphoric feeling I had when winning, something I actually did quite often. However, as I became more reckless the losses mounted up and began to be difficult to hide. This led to my having a bank account and credit card that Melody knew nothing about. I was living a dual life which added to my stress. All of this was happening while I became more physically incapacitated and withdrawn due to the regular personal attacks, surgeries, visits to the ER, and emotional wounds.

My relationship with my birth mom was still less than positive and caused additional heartache. One of the things I wanted to do was forgive the major who had molested me when I was thirteen. However, once I located an address for him, my thoughts became sinister as opposed to righteous. At the time, we had a shotgun that broke down into two pieces and reloaded our own shells. One afternoon I wrapped the shotgun in a blanket, gathered several shells, and placed them into my car. I began driving north, first stopping at the casino and then drove towards Kent, where the major lived. I had every intention of paying him back for all the pain he had caused both Jim and me. I wanted him to suffer at my hands as I had suffered at his. These thoughts were straight from the pit of Hell. It seemed like any rational notion was chased from my mind and replaced by ideas of striking back in vengeance. I was past the point of concern regarding the consequences. However, about an hour after leaving the casino my thoughts began to clear. Everything hit me and it was like living a nightmare but this time, instead of being the victim, I would be the perpetrator. I could not believe I was actually on the highway with malicious intent against another individual. What was I doing?

I knew I could not carry through with my plans. I pulled to the side of I-5 just south of Olympia as the tears poured out of my reddened eyes for what seemed like an eternity. Once again, I turned towards heaven and asked God why I had to suffer so much pain. I begged Him for relief. I accused Him of being forgetful. It was one of the most honest times I had before God and with myself. For the first time, I was totally broken. I saw just how evil my heart still was despite following Him for years. It was clear that I had no real power or control. Any arrogance from my abilities was immediately stripped away as I looked into my heart. Although I called Melody to let her know I was coming home, I cannot tell you much about the conversation or the trip back. Part of the problem was that despite our having been married for over twenty years at the time, I had never shared anything about what the major had done to me. How would I explain what took me to this point? How could she understand the depth of the pain I had carried all of those years?

It was perhaps the most difficult conversation I had with Melody because I was not sure how she would respond. Would she be angry at me for not sharing earlier? Would she want to leave me knowing I had intentions to actually murder someone in cold blood? Could she understand all the pain I had endured? I was on the precipice of life and wanted to end it there. I did not want to address any of this but also knew that the only way to find a measure of peace, comfort, and forgiveness, was by being totally honest. When I arrived home, I told her all of it; what the major did to me, my bitterness and hatred of my parents, the disappointment with God, as well as the gambling and hidden debt. I did not sleep that night as I figured Melody and the boys would reject me outright, and I would lose everything. I fully expected they would be gone in the morning.

That night, I made the decision to end my life using various narcotics I had from my many surgeries. I wanted to find peace and felt it would not be found in this life. Much of the following days are still lost in my mind as I took the pills and ended up in the psych ward at a local hospital where I would stay for a week. This was the lowest point in my life. I was now cut off from everyone, in a secured area of the hospital where cameras watched me 24/7, and even my clothes were taken and replaced with scrubs.

This was a temporary holding facility to evaluate individuals, so the staff repeatedly asked the same questions throughout the day and took lengthy notes. They seemed to care but it was from a distance. It was a cold, sterile, impersonal place that in many ways, enhanced the loneliness and despair that brought me there in the first place.

All of us placed in the psychiatric ward were encouraged to relax by listening to music, writing our thoughts, and even coloring in books. While the last one seemed silly to me, I found music and writing to be helpful, so I wrote about my experience in the ward, what brought me to the point I wanted to quit living, and my confusion about how God seemed so distant. I listened to peaceful music and tried to picture myself at the beach listening to the waves. It was there that I was finally able to be honest not only with those around me but also with myself. It was while in this secluded, mysterious, part of the hospital, a place where people who are desperate sometimes find themselves, that I was able to begin my journey towards healing.

After leaving, several things happened quickly. The first was telling the church leaders where I had been and why, and then I stepped down from my role as a pastor. The next decision was not the wisest but because of the comments from two of the leaders, I decided not to attend church any longer. Maybe those elders were right. Had I been redeemed? Could I be restored and find healing? It would be almost a year before I realized that though some had hurt me deeply with their comments after my suicide attempt, God never quit on me. Just as before, He was there. He called for me to return to Him. He sought to restore me both for my own sake as well as that of the Kingdom!

Finally, I began weekly counseling with a Christian clinical psychologist I had visited before this series of events. Although he was instrumental in helping me learn new patterns of communication and responses to stress, his most important work was helping me get into a military PTSD live-in facility at Cedar Mills, on the west side of Portland.

Several months had passed since my stay in the psych ward at Adventist Medical Center, but I recognized that a longer-term program could be extremely helpful. After talking it over with my wife, I decided to complete the paperwork. Shortly after they received the application, I received a call saying there was an opening the following Sunday and that I would be there between four to six weeks. As Sunday approached, I began to wonder if it was worth it or if I should just live my life the best I could.

What finally helped me go was reading Ephesians again. I accepted the premise that God loved me and if He was really directing things, then maybe He planned this all along. I asked Him to help me. My prayers were those of a desperate man. I understood that my feeble attempts to escape pain and avoid difficult conversations had not worked. I needed His help. I needed a better understanding of my mental state due to all the abuse I had endured and how the stressful roles I had in different careers exacerbated the situation. I also needed help with my frequent bouts of depression and anxiety.

When I arrived at the facility, I was pleasantly surprised to learn we were allowed to wear civilian clothes and we were not restricted to our rooms. Instead, there was a common area where we could visit, work on assignments, or just sit and listen to others. There was no television as the staff wanted our focus to be on healing and not be distracted. Each of us had a roommate, and mine was Carl. He was an Oregon National Guard sergeant who was burned over about twenty percent of his body, had pins holding one leg together, and had healed from a broken back which happened when his vehicle hit an Improvised Explosive Device (IED) in Iraq.

Many people are unaware that many of the units fighting in both Afghanistan and Iraq came from the National Guard. Since there is no real military presence in Oregon, there are no military hospitals. As members of the Guard returned from their deployments, it was civilians who had to coordinate care for their physical and mental health. Since there was nothing available to handle the onslaught of PTSD cases, they created the program at Cedar Mills for individuals from the Guard and on active duty, as well as those who were retired.

At first, I felt like I did not belong there since I had not been in combat. However, as I began working on my assignments, I learned two important things about PTSD. The first was that it is about our response to trauma and that the brain does not delineate traumatic events between peace time and wartime. Trauma is trauma. I wept for these young men as they shared about their experiences in combat and how it impacted their lives. Like me, most had addiction issues with everything from drugs and alcohol to porn and gambling. Prior to our arrival at Cedar Mills, each of us was active in some sort of program to help us avoid our escapes from reality and for me, that was Gamblers Anonymous. All of us struggled with developing relationships. Each of us fought our battles into the night when we relived moments that haunted and taunted us. All of us were broken by our experiences and longed for some measure of peace and some sort of a normal life. All of us cried unashamedly each day and hugged one another while we fought our own ongoing battles.

Throughout the four weeks at this facility, the medical teams, comprised of medical doctors, psychiatrists, social workers, and counselors tried different medications and techniques to prevent, or at least reduce, my nightmares. However, many of the prescription meds only made me more anxious because I would have no recollection of anything after taking them. We finally decided to use Trazadone and Prazosin, but they did not alleviate the ongoing nighttime horrors. When I left the facility, I had identified my triggers and stressors, understood more about how trauma affects the brain, and was rested. My time at Cedar Mills helped me work regular jobs even while the nightmares remained. While horrible, they were the lesser of two evils and I figured that at least I had more tools in my chest to function throughout each day.

My transition back home felt awkward on many levels because I had been learning a new way of addressing things, but Melody and Andy were not sure what to expect. The first few days found me pretty withdrawn and ashamed about all I had put them through. However, as we began to learn this new dance, a new sense of normal began to take shape. It was a difficult time for all of us, but we kept getting back up each day seeking to navigate life together. Although helpful, my time at Cedar Mills did not bring about the deeper changes that needed to occur in my mind or heart.

Once home, I made the decision to find another church and begin attending again. Both Mel and I settled on Cornerstone, a church that met in an elementary gym and whose elders seemed to fulfill their roles. I soon discovered that the pastor, Barry Arnold, was not a stranger to chronic, debilitating, pain. As such, I found a kindred spirit who not only understood some of the dynamics of how pain impacted every aspect of life, but also accepted me. Mel and I came to appreciate this body of believers and connected with others through the various community groups. In many ways, it was a refreshing change that I needed to rekindle my love for God.

I also continued my weekly counseling sessions until my counselor retired. After that, I tried to gut it out on my own, but that did not work. I tried working with another counselor but while he was polite, we did not make any real connection, so I continued enduring the ongoing mental anguish that was only becoming worse. Throughout this time my physical health continued to decline and my bouts with depression became more regular. These darker times became my constant companion, and the burden was becoming increasingly untenable. I was quickly descending into a very dark, and dangerous, hole.

After four or five surgeries, I began to tire of hospitals and also became numb to their routines and protocols. Having twenty surgical procedures within a short period of time became unbearable. I was becoming desperate and continually asked for prayer. People laid hands on me, anointed me with oil, sent kind notes, and patted my back. Some well-meaning individuals even suggested this was the result of sin in my life and told me I needed to pray more. These comments only reinforced the possibility that I had gone too far for even God to use, or work with, me. It was not long before I felt like nothing more than a prayer project, a burden for others, and began to shut myself off from them and try to put on a happy face. Somewhere along the way, I had a revelation; what if I was not supposed to be healed? What if God wanted to use these things so I could minister to others? What if this was part of His plan for me?

At first these thoughts depressed me because the implications were that I would live a life of physical pain. But slowly, at a seemingly glacial pace, I began to sense that this might be what God had planned. This was both transformative, and freeing. It was only after these thoughts took hold that I began to pray for and with my medical teams in the hospitals and at their offices. When I was laid up, I had many opportunities to just listen to people and hear their stories. It allowed me a greater depth of compassion than I previously had. Suddenly I became aware I was learning to be content and was no longer fighting God. Instead, I sought to understand what He was doing through all of it and asked for guidance and wisdom for direction.

After stepping down as the lead elder at FBC, I became an Assistant Registrar, and then Director of Admissions, at Multnomah University. While the roles were satisfying on many levels, it was not a place that I could stay long term for both personal and professional reasons. I struggled with the cost of higher education in general, but more specifically of

Christian colleges and universities as they often do not have the resources to significantly reduce their overhead costs. This led to my taking positions with the Gresham-Barlow School District first as an Educational Assistant at West Gresham Elementary School and then as the *Career Coordinator* in the College and Career office, which at the time was overseen by the counseling staff, at Gresham High School. I found both extremely rewarding but it was the latter position where I felt most able to encourage and help students and families in their life decisions. I loved the diversity of the student body and found the administration at the district and school levels to be helpful and supportive.

I could help these students because of the many role models throughout my years of school who had stood beside me and showed me a new, better, different, way to live and approach life. I had truly been blessed by each of them. Because of their compassion, I have always believed that whatever I did for a career, and wherever we lived, I had an obligation to come alongside those who were struggling. This has been the compelling mission of my heart and life, a calling that God has uniquely designed for me as I have gone through various trials throughout my life.

As much as I have enjoyed this calling, one problem has regularly come up: boundaries. It was tempting to think of myself as indispensable when assisting others and take on their burdens. Burnout, cynicism, and feelings of being overwhelmed were the result. During my time at Gresham High School, I found myself in this predicament once again. You would think I had learned my lesson about carrying additional burdens when my own also needed to be tended to, but I hadn't. One of my first roles at the high school was supervising an Independent Study seven periods each day. Although some would see this as a time to catch up on reading, I wanted to use the time to get to know the students, listen to their concerns and questions, talk with their teachers when they were struggling, and allow them to bounce ideas off of me on basically any subject. It was not very long before students began talking with me about these things and they brought their friends to me after class when they needed to talk. My role also involved working with new students from around the world who spoke little, or no, English. We would communicate through pictures drawn on a whiteboard and this helped them connect not just with me but other students as well. As these students were given regular class schedules, they would continually come to me and often introduced their parents and siblings to me as well. One of the projects the teacher who taught them English had them complete was writing out their story. When they gave me copies, it was in a reverent manner. It often moved me greatly because I realized this was more than just an assignment, they were revealing their hearts and lives to me. Due to my own experiences overseas, I understood how vulnerable it is to be in a different culture and not be able to communicate. It takes a great deal of courage and energy just to keep getting up and going out each day and yet these students did just that!.

I made myself available to help both at school as well as on weekends and evenings by meeting them in coffee shops or restaurants. I also discovered other areas where I could help, showing them how to do taxes for free, helping parents get their ITN numbers to file their taxes, and helping students and their parents work with immigration officials to address issues. This included getting Senator Ron Wyden involved in a case related to one student's parents. The issue was resolved within a couple weeks of his involvement when all of the "lost" paperwork was suddenly discovered, and they received their Permanent Resident status. Helping these families has been some of the most rewarding moments of my life.

One of the most precious trainings I was allowed to attend while at the high school was the Trauma Informed Practices conferences. I did not look at any student the same after these sessions as it was clear that a large number of our students had been severely traumatized by everything imaginable. These things began impacting my own life as it became clearer that not only was I not able to fix things, but the counselors and social workers were also unable to stop the daily triage of students and their needs. I marveled at their resiliency and have a great deal of respect for the women who were in these roles. One of the main differences I noticed was their ability to separate themselves from the situations even though they had a deep love for the students no matter who they were. They modeled boundaries as well as how to encourage others, like me, who were sometimes worn down by it all. Seldom have I had the opportunity to work with such caring people who sought to come along the neediest.

When I was in junior high and high school, neither of my parents attended any events other than those associated with bagpiping. Aside from breaking my speech and debate trophies, my parents showed little interest in coming to observe me in my element. As a father, I tried to make it to as many activities as I could with Rob and Andy. If they were into hunting, I learned how to hunt. If it was computer games, I made time to play them – even when I was not that good! When Andy became enthralled with the Marvel Universe and Star Wars, I became an avid reader and watched all the movies with him. These were times that created strong bonds and positive memories that has allowed us to remain close throughout the years despite everything that has happened.

While working in the high school, I made a point to attend various activities, from sporting events, to musicals, and concerts, as often as possible because I knew some of the students would have no one there to cheer them on. It was not mandated, or even strongly encouraged, by anyone that staff members do this. However, I knew the loneliness of not having any supporters present during these events. I wanted to be there for the students who had no one else. These activities gave me additional opportunities to connect with students, staff, parents, and families. Watching these students outside of the normal school day often brought a lump in my throat and filled my own heart with joy because they grateful I was there for them. My own life was enriched and some of the pain from my own experiences began to be replaced with these new, wonderful, images of being the one cheering for those without anyone else to praise them.

At different points between 2006 and the spring of 2020, my counselors and several doctors encouraged me to consider either changing careers or working fewer hours. I could not see myself doing either so I continued working and tried to be a positive role model for those I encountered. There were many days when it was all I could do to just keep up the façade of having it together because many areas of my life were deteriorating. On two occasions I actually sat in the office of different counselors at the high school and cried because a student had died in an accident. It was becoming more difficult to contain my own emotions because I had been addressing my own traumatic past as well with a new counselor and different approach.

Chapter 16
The Road to Wholeness

During this same timeframe my wife and I became friends with a woman, Linda Hill, at the church we attended. She had been a counselor for years and continues working with women who have been traumatized. As she came to know me and more about my own story, she wanted to help not only by being there but also through recommending a counselor that worked with people who have experienced trauma.

For over twenty years, I have had a recurring nightmare four to five nights a week. I would break out in sweats, shake uncontrollably, scream, and cry throughout the ordeals. In these nightmares I was held down and hacked into pieces by my parents and/or the major. These violent night terrors attacked with a fury and if I was able to go back to sleep, they continued where they left off. If I had communication with my biological mom, or others that had unwarranted, harsh, words for me, I knew what awaited me when I tried to sleep. At the time I was taking heavy doses of prescription medications, including Prazosin and Trazadone, but they had little effect.

After my requests for prayer, Linda mentioned there was a counselor who might be able to help me move out of this cycle of nightmares. I called him the next day and, while he was extremely busy, he rearranged his schedule to see me on Tuesday evening. Both Mel and I were anxious as my darker days were becoming more frequent. I was becoming more agitated for longer periods of time, and our interactions were becoming increasingly difficult. In short, we were both desperate and needed help to move on not only as individuals but as a couple as well.

This counselor explained the premise of a unique approach to counseling called, *Eye Movement Desensitization and Reprocessing* (EMDR). He also shared about how it had helped many who have struggled from the debilitating impact of traumatic events in their lives. The only concern he expressed was that he was already at capacity and could not accept any other patients at the time. Those words sucked the hope out of my heart and soul. I wondered if this was what drowning people might feel like when a life ring was thrown to them and then it disappeared under the waves. As despair began to take hold, he shared there was only one other counselor he would feel comfortable with me seeing, Mary Jane (MJ) Wilt. Once we were home, I called MJ to see if we could meet, hoping it could be soon.

She returned my call on Wednesday and set an appointment for Thursday. It was another life ring tossed to me while I struggled to stay afloat in the tumultuous sea that engulfed me. I was nervous, hopeful, and excited about how our first meeting would go. When she opened her door, I recognized her from when I was the pastor at FBC. This set me at ease, and we were able to catch up on what had transpired in the intervening years. Part of the reason that I did not recognize her name is that she had been divorced but was remarried, a journey she speaks about in her book, *Grounds for Marriage.*

I was immediately caught up with MJ's calm demeanor, focused eyes that conveyed compassion and care, and her soft voice. She is a believer who is focused on living real, authentic, Christianity and surrounding herself with others who wanted to serve others and not be part of a social club. I must admit, I chuckled a little about a blue streak she had in her hair but came to see this as her statement about being OK with being different. Over the next few weeks, I had numerous assignments. They began to open many wounds that had not, or at least not properly, healed. It was the beginning of an excruciatingly painful years-long process.

Unlike any counseling office I had been in before, MJ had an entire wall that was a whiteboard, and we used it often. We drew family diagrams and discussed all the various interactions and relational aspects between different members of my family so that she had a solid framework about areas of concern and what I had lived through. This process was so intense that I was literally sobbing both during and after each session, while driving home, and at many times during the days that followed my appointments. But I was desperate. I had to trust that the benefit would outweigh the discomfort in the end. The pain associated with these assignments reminded me of something Melody shared after both of our sons had been born; "Yes, childbirth is painful, but we have something wonderful in the end."

Each week I completed my assignments and brought additional notes as the exercises usually brought up additional issues. One of the questions that MJ often asked was if anyone else was present when "X" event happened? I often wondered if she had really heard me, but knew she had a reason for asking the question, so I did not respond with sarcasm or anything other than curiosity as to where it was leading. After several months, and before doing any actual EMDR work, MJ had me select which of the issues was having the most impact on my life. This was an easy choice. If I could somehow get control of one specific nightmare, then I could get some sleep. As we went over the actual incident that seemed to have caused this nightly terror, I became scared of what might happen if EMDR did not help. I really felt this was my last hope.

When I arrived the following week, MJ had me try different types of stimuli that would be used during the actual EMDR process. After trying the various options, I chose to use a set of small headphones that would allow me to hear a rhythmic beeping. Once we determined the tone, volume, and specific spacing of the beeps, MJ asked me to describe the details of the incident that seemed to have caused this specific nightmare. This is nothing like hypnosis because I was fully aware of everything happening and, after just a few moments, I no longer even heard the beeps and was totally focused on our discussion.

Often, impressions and emotional connections to traumatic events create such strong neuropaths that there is no room to address or revisit the actual facts. However, as we talked, I recalled some very specific details from the nightmares and the incident. For the first time, I recalled my dad's blue sweater, but I had not ever recalled it prior to this session. When I went home and talked with Melody about it, she asked, "Don't you remember he always had on that blue sweater?" I had forgotten it as my focus had been on the intense anger in his eyes, his blowing smoke into my face, and his laughter. What he was wearing did not even appear on my radar. In fact, several other things came to light that I had not even considered before this session. This did not make it easier, but it began countering my emotional responses to both this nightmare and the actual events.

These sessions were exceptionally draining, difficult, and took their own emotional toll. In fact, one of my good friends, Matt Moffat, and I met weekly during this time and not only listened to my explanation of how the sessions went but also saw the growing fatigue in my spirit and body. He told me, "This better work because it is hard to sit and watch what this is doing to you." He was not upset at MJ but was not sure about EMDR and concerned at how much energy it was using from my near-empty emotional bank. To his credit, he walked through this part of the valley with me and checked in often to see how I was doing as we cried, prayed, and shared lunches together. His presence became an anchor for me during this time and was a huge source of encouragement. Like most counseling, the results are not immediately apparent, but my approach to this area of life *was* changing.

Our sessions continued as we worked through things that arose during the week as well as the longer-term things that continued to adversely affect my life. A great deal of time was spent addressing what it means to forgive someone and whether that meant the forgiven individual had to be allowed back into one's life or not. Over the years, I had been advised by pastors and other counselors that the answer to this was yes. Consequently, I was frustrated and bitter about being hurt again and never making headway. Beginning in February 2019, MJ helped me work through this and spent almost twenty-one months with EMDR and counseling focused on relational issues. Part of this process included writing letters to each of my parents, as well as Melody.

The first letter was to my dad and honestly, even reading it today, it is clear there was a great deal of anger and bitterness in the tone and actual words. My dad was as aggressive in his actions towards me as I was passive and frightened of him when I was a child. Because of this, I made the decision to write as though he could not move from a chair and had to listen. I wrote it through deep sobs of regret and sadness about what might have been. However, it was the first time I had ever verbalized what I really felt. This brought a real sense of calm and peace about our relationship, something I had never experienced.

It also seemed so contrary to my personal ethos about trying to speak only things that were uplifting and encouraging. However, that was part of the purpose of the assignment. Throughout the decades following Christ, I had bought into the idea that it is sinful to be angry about things. But I was angry about many things, and not speaking what I held in my heart had become an additional burden I often carried alone.

This three-page letter took almost a month to complete. When it was finished, I was totally spent and yet sleep still remained elusive to me.

Since the assignment had stirred up the intensity of the nightmares, MJ and I looked to addressing some of the issues Mel and I have struggled with throughout our marriage. Because of my confidence and trust in MJ, not only as a counselor, but as a fellow sojourner, I spoke freely. I shared about my struggles with trying to live the Christian life as others have defined it and how much of a burden that had been for me. The church was not normally a place where I felt a part of things as so many seemed to have such wonderful, easy, joyous lives. There was only right and wrong, black and white, things you did and things you did not do. It seemed that rules about dancing, playing cards, having a beer, or having tattoos were the real measure of whether one was a Christian. I often felt like I did not measure up.

In my discussions with MJ, I shared that in many ways I blamed Melody's inability to show affection, or let others see that she cared about them, came from her strong conservative upbringing. As our sessions continued, it became clear that I was the one choosing to accept what I thought others wanted to see and this was what dictated how I lived much of my faith. Mary Jane asked, "What stops you from finding a different group of believers that aligns more to what you believe is important?" This was the first time I had considered doing anything like looking for a place where I could both serve and be with people who have experienced their own difficult journey in life. My response was, "Melody would never go for that," to which she replied, "So what?"

Was it really that easy? Could I really make a choice to worship differently, or even attend a different church than her? While considering this possibility, I confessed to Mel that I placed a lot of blame on her for spiritual things. This led to my asking her more questions so that I could understand her views on various aspects of faith. I began to ask questions about how she handled stresses at her home of origin as I was beginning to realize that if my home of origin impacted me, then hers must have impacted her life as well. I prayed for help understanding the pain Melody carried from her own experiences. I wanted to grasp what I needed to learn from what she had shared.

One day, while walking on the treadmill at the gym, I had a very different thought. At first it seemed fragmentary, and though I sensed it went together, I could not see how. Over the next several days, I conversed with God about the confusion I felt when praying about this and then it hit me, "Mel tries to control things and cleans the house when she feels there is no control over other things." Slowly, I began to weep silently as I slowed the pace on treadmill, but within moments I was overwhelmed with the reality that much of Melody's responses related not only to my emotional ups and downs, suicide attempts, previous gambling addiction, and never knowing what to expect from me but also from her years growing up in her parents' home.

Melody's oldest sister had shared with me that when their parents argued, Melody would retreat into her room to clean and decorate it. As I showered at the gym, I was once again reminded of the marvelous truth that God cleanses us, He had cleansed me. He continues cleaning my heart and will do so through eternity. With these things ruminating in my mind, I decided that instead of heading to work after my workout I needed to go home first. When I arrived, Melody was reading in her chair and was surprised to see me. I literally knelt at her feet sobbing as I shared and confessed all of this to her. It was one of the few times I have seen her really show emotion, and her tears mingled with mine as we held each other. Her sobs were of one who felt more fully understood and connected, perhaps for the first time in years and mine were because God answered my prayer in a most unexpected manner.

Throughout the first 25 years of our marriage, I was on the road for both the Army and Air Force. At the time I did not give it much thought. I felt that as long as I was growing in my faith, coaching whenever possible, participating in activities with the boys, doing more difficult chores around the house, and providing a good living, then everything was great.

Although I did not have a full picture of what a marriage should be like, a large part of the image was starting to be filled in. Throughout our marriage, my heart softened to what I found in the Bible, as did my speech, intensity, and selfish attitude. Despite all of these changes, I recognized there were areas needing additional work so I read many books about love languages, connecting with a spouse, personality types, and felt these would correct the problems. The reality is that while they helped, the underlying issues stemmed from our individual experiences. Over the years, Mel expressed frustration about counseling as she felt it was about learning how to deal with me and my issues.

Many of the areas where I struggled were out there for the world to see. However, I came to understand that other, subtle, sins are just as grievous to the Lord. Things like pride, malice, anger, bitterness, lusts, arrogance, gossip, gluttony, and jealousies are just as wrong, but they sometimes seem to be allowed within some Christian circles. What little energy I could devote towards improvement could not be focused on Mel or others, as there was plenty of room for growth in my own heart and life.

This is why I continued to work on issues like these over the next few years in my sessions with MJ. Each of them allowed me to look into my own heart and address deeper issues that had interfered with my relationships. Although MJ and I discussed various aspects of our marriage, we always returned to the relational issues I had with my parents, the sexual assault on both my brother and me, as well as my not being able to prevent Jim's suicide. Although I shared about my dad first, it was addressing the issues between my mother and me that presented the most difficulties. MJ asked me to do the same type of letter for my mother as I had for my dad but for whatever reason, I could not allow myself to write with the same tone as I had with my dad. After reading my first attempted letter to my mom aloud, MJ silently clapped her hands sarcastically and said, "That was very, academic. Now I need you to write another letter, but this time write what you would really tell her." Sadly, it would take many months before I could complete that assignment. This was not because MJ wanted to move on to other areas, but rather, because Mel and I were struggling more as the nightmares became more intense and I was exhausted, with a short fuse.

In any long-term relationship, each party learns the "steps to the dance." When one party make changes, a new dance is created and inevitably, toes get stepped on and feelings are hurt. All of the counseling, meditation on the Scriptures, and continual conviction about areas needing to be changed began affecting the way I lived. One Sunday afternoon, before uniting our two families under one roof, Andy and his family were visiting for a late lunch. At some point Melody made a statement that something had to be done right then. Instead of the normal, "OK," I replied, "Not now, I will do it after the kids leave." Andy literally stood, almost shell-shocked, in the kitchen and said, "That is the first time in my life I have ever heard you tell mom no to anything." It was not a rancorous statement. Instead, he saw a different dance step and was actually pleasantly surprised. I was learning to make some boundaries and decisions on things that were not urgent.

Within a few years I was able to express concerns without going to my normal default position of "I could not be right, she has been a Christian longer than me," or, "I deserve this because of things I have done in the past." This allowed me to discover my own voice not only in conversations as a couple, but also in many other relationships as well.

Every individual brings baggage into each relationship. Although it is much easier to address difficult issues as they arise when the parties are open, the task becomes almost impossible when one, or more, of the parties has not been honest. Unfortunately, by not being fully transparent with Melody from the earliest days of our relationship about the full extent of the abuse I experienced, I carried this burden alone and many of my responses to situations over the years did not make sense to her or our sons. Things like not wanting the boys to stay overnight at friends or being hypervigilant when other men were around them made no sense without the additional context. Were it not for Melody's strong faith and love for both the Lord and me, our marriage would have just been another casualty of the abuse I endured as a child.

While I continued with my counseling, I often wondered if I would ever be emotionally or physically healthy. I knew enough to realize that the regular nightmares, medications for trying to control my nerve pain each day and to help me sleep, coupled with seriously considering suicide were not indicators of a healthy life. However, there would be two defining moments that would change my view of the world, my traumatic experiences, and God.

The first occurred immediately following a surgery to put rods into my lower back. Although the surgery itself went according to plan, when they inserted the catheter, it pierced my urethra and urine seeped into my abdomen. This resulted in my contracting *E. coli*. As my fever continued to rise, the doctors ran numerous tests and cultures to discover what caused the issue. While they waited for the cultures to return, they administered copious amounts of very strong antibiotics to attack whatever was assaulting my system. Fortunately, after an additional week in the hospital, I was able to go home. I was physically and emotionally drained and weaker than I could recall after any of the other surgeries I had prior to this. However, what was to happen next became a medical life and death battle as my body fought a new, and more potent, enemy *Clostridiodes difficile* or *C. diff* for short.

Since the recovery from the actual surgery was about six weeks, Mel and I went to the beach where I am most able to relax. Our plan was for me to lay in front of the window where I could enjoy the ocean, breezes, sounds of the birds, and sunsets. However, after dinner on the first night, I went into a semi-conscious state and was rushed by ambulance to the hospital in Seaside, Oregon. Within a couple hours, I was rushed back to a Portland hospital and then placed in the ICU for several days because my systems were shutting down as the doctors struggled to get things stabilized. Later, I asked one of the doctors why I could not speak, my vision was blurred, and I could not hear during some of this time in the ICU. He explained that my body was shutting everything down and keeping only the critical things going. He also told me that there were moments when they really did not know if I would pull through because my blood pressure dropped for significant periods several times during my stay.

I have only three memories of that time and all were from the latter part of my stay. One was of a man wearing a gown and mask, sitting by my hospital bed, reading the Psalms. It was like nothing I had heard before. The words brought peace to my mind as I tried to understand where I was and how I got there. That man was one of our pastors, Joel Woodard. Those were the first words I heard in four days, and they were the seeds that created a desire to understand more about the Psalms. However, it would be another year before I decided to actually read through all 150 of them.

At first, I just read through them. When I completed this, I decided to rewrite each of them into the first person. Once I did this, they became personal and real for me. It was as if blinders came off and I was standing in the full radiance of the sun. Even as I completed this, I wanted more but did not know how to proceed. After a short time, I decided it might be good to pray through what I wrote about each Psalm. The prayers were accomplished by reading the actual Psalm followed by my first-person rendition, and then closing my eyes and typing. This process took almost four and a half years. Through it, my heart softened, and I gained a new perspective of God. As I reflected on all that God had been doing in my life I was often left in tears. These moments of reflection brought me to my knees. I praised Him for His great compassion, care, and mercy towards me. Although the original intent of the project was just to record my thoughts to share with our family, it became a book entitled *My Journey in Psalms, a First-Person Rendition of Psalms and Associated Prayers*.

My time in the Psalms strengthened my faith and allowed me to break free from my self-imposed mold of what it meant to practice my beliefs, serve others, and arrange the priorities in my life. Just as counseling was beginning to give me courage to begin a new dance with my relationships, the time in Psalms redefined how I approach God, prayed, and interact with others. They had not, however, removed the nightmares, anxiety, darker days, or times of depression. But God had another gift that would revolutionize every aspect of my life and bring even greater freedom and healing.

Chapter 17

The Truman Show

Throughout my military career, our family was often the happy owners of dogs. However, because there are waiting lists for base housing, we often had to live in apartments when we first arrived at our next assignment. Many times there were strict rules associated with having dogs and we struggled watching our boys hurt when we needed to give the dogs away. So, we became a cat family. I was surprised how affectionate some cats could be and came to enjoy felines. Although I still longed for a dog, I normally put the thought out of my mind.

However, after retiring from the Air Force one of my counselors I suggested looking into obtaining a PTSD service dog. In the spring of 2019, after much discussion with Melody, coupled with the knowledge that the nightmares were not decreasing despite various approaches for help, we decided to pursue this option.

As I searched the internet, it quickly became apparent that this option was extremely expensive since the dogs themselves ranged from just under $40,000 to around $45,000. The organizations that trained these Service Dogs had their own requirements and since I did not meet some of those, my options narrowed to about ten organizations. Almost all of them were out of state which meant the travel, as well as hotel and meals while getting trained with the dog, would increase the costs. The process involved being placed on a waiting list, spending one to two years raising money, and once the funds were raised, being placed on another list before actually receiving a dog. For many organizations, this meant a three to five year waiting period before any training began. Like many who struggle with PTSD, I was desperate for help, and would do whatever to make this happen. I could raise the money, but would I be able to go on living this way for another few years?

The application process involves a great deal of paperwork, videos of your home and yard, and questionnaires for one's spouse, friends, counselor(s), and doctor(s). These requirements would be followed by phone interviews and in-person meetings before any decision was made. Although I completed applications with several organizations, I only heard back from one group that conducted training in San Diego. They looked like a solid organization, and were close to Melody's sister, which would be a great help when I went and trained with a dog. Their staff were enthusiastic, interested in the specific issues associated with my application, compassionate, and professional. During a talk with one of them I asked why I could not begin training once I raised the money? She explained that it related both to when specific dogs would be available as well as the rules associated with being a non-profit organization as opposed to a private business. While it helped me understand the rationale, I did not look forward to the long wait. Even with this concern, I wanted to believe that God would provide the money for me to receive a dog sooner as opposed to later.

During the spring and fall semesters in 2019 my stress levels remained high. In May of 2019, a recent graduate from the high school died in an accident the week before the anniversary of my brother's suicide, my workload was going to increase because my office partner decided not to return in the fall, and there were rising tensions in our home, exacerbated by my concerns about whether I could actually raise the funds for a service dog. Looking back, I was not fully convinced God would answer my prayer, nor did I feel like I deserved such a grace.

The day after the student died, I realized he was the brother of a girl I had known from my earlier work at West Gresham Elementary. Whereas she was a student at Gresham High School herself, my heart broke when I saw her in the hallway, and I struggled to function throughout the weeks following the accident. Although counselors were available for students to get help processing their grief, I could not contain my own tears so I poured out my heart to two of the counselors. At first, I was embarrassed but they allowed my brokenness to be heard and shared. Their friendship and compassion helped me make it through that time, but I was at the precipice of despair much like I experienced after Jim died.

As the school year began in the fall, my existence seemed to have been reduced to continual nerve pain, nightmares, causing pain for Melody and the boys, and struggling to live out the discoveries I found while studying the Psalms. I wanted more than this and began a descent back into the darkness that had swallowed me earlier in life. At the same time, I found that working with the students was the very thing I needed as a counterweight to the darker thoughts. Connecting with many who struggled with issues similar to those I wrestled with while in high school allowed me to speak into their lives. Sometimes, they just needed someone to listen to them as they shared everything from heartaches to achievements. This is what I was built to do, and yet I was continually asking myself, "Can I really help them?" While work filled me with a sense of purpose, it was not helping me move away from my own growing depression and thoughts of ending my life.

On October 15, I received an email from a woman named Michelle, who was associated with a group called *Paws Assisting Veterans* (***PAVE***). She wanted to talk with me about submitting the full application for one of their PTSD Service Dogs. Although I shared about the group I was already working with, I thought it might warrant further discussion so I reached out to their client advisor, Cheryl Mulick, who would work with me through the actual application process. When I asked where they were located, she told me they were in Boring. I could not believe this because they were literally only about thirteen miles from where we lived!

In January, Cheryl came to meet us for our "Home Visit," and share more information about their program and expectations. She was accompanied by a beautiful black lab named Bullet. Throughout her almost three-hour visit, I was amazed at how well-mannered Bullet was and found myself staring at him. I wanted to pet him but knew that would be inappropriate. Cheryl asked questions like, "Do you prefer a male or female dog? Is there a specific breed or size you are looking for? Do you prefer one color over another?" My answer to each question was always the same, "I really do not care. I need help." When it came time for Melody and me to ask questions, we had only two, how much money would be needed and how long until I might receive a dog.

Even as I asked these questions, my heart trembled, my voice and body were shaking, and tears welled up in my eyes because I expected the growing hope to be dashed. However, just as the email was a surprise, so too were Cheryl's answers. She explained there were no costs for their program or dog as they relied solely on grants and donations, and that if I was accepted into their program, a dog might be ready to begin training with me in a few months' time. I thought I heard wrong and asked for clarification. My tears flowed as she reaffirmed there was no financial cost to us and that she was talking about a timeframe much earlier than 2021.

As we ended the visit, Cheryl asked if I would like to officially meet Bullet and my heart melted. Holding his face in my hands, rubbing his silky back, and imagining him as a companion overwhelmed all my senses and left me wondering if God was actually going to answer my prayers. Once she left, Mel and I sat together on the couch and sobbed. Was this a real lifeline amidst the raging storm that was swallowing me? Could I allow myself to even hope again? Might this be one of God's clearest demonstrations of His love and compassion? As I went to bed, my tears again flowed freely. However, for one of the first times in my life, these were tears of hope. I really sensed God's presence in a way that I had never felt, or understood, before. This does not mean I was without fear that this might not work out, but I wanted, needed, to grasp this lifeline.

While I continued gathering the required documents and letters, Cheryl invited me over to see where she was located, how she works with the dogs, and just get to know one another better. It was clear she was a woman of great faith in Christ who saw her work as a real calling. Prior to this work she had trained show dogs for decades but once she heard about the goal of PAVE, her course and priorities changed. Before long we became good friends, and my hopes continued to rise because I did not think she would spend this much time with me if they did not want to work with me.

One serious question that concerned me related to how the school and district would respond to having a service dog in the school. All of the administrators were very helpful, and we worked through the process to make this happen. Whereas this was as new to them as it was to me, they had basic questions about when and where the dog would relieve himself, how we would notify parents, staff, and students, where we would need signage, and what the dog would be doing when he was with me. Their support made things easier than I ever imagined and they found ways to make this work and meet the needs of all of their constituents. Once their questions were answered and we had a plan in place, I was told I would begin training on Monday, March 16th!

Prior to that day, there was a large manual I had to read and understand. It outlined the basic commands I would use; laws regarding service dogs; the differences between emotional, therapy, and service dogs; and detailed information about how dogs work. In January and February, I was also taking saliva samples when things were going OK, when I was stressed, after nightmares, when relaxing, or immediately after episodic events associated with my PTSD responses. These were used to train the dog I would receive as to what he should do when specific scents were detected.

I was so excited the evening before beginning training that I could not sleep. After completing the written test Cheryl asked, "Are you ready to meet your dog?" I was! As we walked to the building where the training took place, she told me that while they originally planned on Bullet becoming my dog, the more they considered my needs, it was apparent he would not be the best fit. This made me wonder if I was going to be given a dog that was second rate instead of one of their 'normal' dogs? As I prepared myself for what lay beyond the door leading to the training area, I kept reminding myself that this was part of God's answer to decades of crying out to Him and I needed to be thankful. Once inside, I saw a cream-colored lab tethered and lying on a mat while Cheryl introduced me to Truman. Although he was a lab, I still had a little sadness about Bullet. However, within a few minutes of working with him, I could sense that he was figuring me out. That's when I realized he was already responding to my body's changing chemistry that told him I was stressed. From that moment on, it was clear that he was part of God's answer to my prayers.

Throughout our long days of training, I felt bad for Truman because he knew the commands, but I often used the wrong one, the incorrect intonation, or a different cadence. Slowly, we began moving from simple commands to more complex ones. Despite my awkwardness and timidity, Truman and I were bonding. After the first week, I was allowed to take him home for the weekend to introduce him to our home and family. While I was excited, I also felt much like I did when we first brought our oldest son home from the hospital. Would he adjust? Where would he sleep? How would Melody adjust with Truman in the house? All of these questions left me drained, but I would do anything to make this work.

I decided to have him on the bed with me while I slept instead of on the dog bed I had purchased. Like so many evenings over the last two decades, I had the regular, violent, nightmares. However, Truman did exactly what he was trained to do and woke me up before I got too far into them. At first, I was surprised by his cold nose tapping my cheek, but then clung to him and cried deeps sobs of hope and joy. As I pushed my face into his soft fur my breathing aligned with his, and I calmed down. This experience happened three more times during that first weekend and each time my confidence in Truman skyrocketed. The only unfortunate thing was that he was extremely tired during the daytime as he was working hard throughout the graveyard shift.

When I returned for additional training on Monday, Cheryl explained that due to COVID and the shutting down of almost everything, we would only be able to complete a portion of the training needed to become certified. As my eyes widened, I feared she was going to say something like, "We will have to wait until everything is open before we can allow Truman to be with you." Instead, she said we would do some training at Costco and that I would be taking Truman home with me at the end of the week. I could not contain my joy and bounced around like Tigger in *Winnie the Pooh*!

Although much of the work focused on my relationship with Truman, Cheryl had also endeared herself to my family and me. As we talked, I discovered a kindred spirit and our friendship deepened. I did not expect anything other than a

Service Dog, but I gained a sister and friend who has become an important part of my life. Her patience and prayers allowed me to practice, and refine, techniques that would soon become second nature.

Many people do not understand the differences between a pet, an emotional service, therapy, or service dog. Service dogs perform specific tasks, conduct natures business, and work all while on leash. Everything is scheduled and food is tightly regulated to ensure they maintain the correct weight and remain healthy. At home, they do not wander around the house or yard or do their own thing. With few exceptions, a service dog is a 24/7companion. It takes years of training before a dog is able to function in this capacity as well as many additional months for the handler and dog to become a solid team and be fully bonded. The results have been the miraculous answer to decades of prayers.

Receiving Truman at the beginning of the COVID pandemic has been perhaps one of the most remarkable aspects of the whole process. The pandemic brought a whole new type of stress into everyone's lives across the globe and would remain longer than almost anyone thought possible. Normally, when additional, or new, stresses come into my life, darker times of despair follow, and my nightmares become more intense. As such, I was afraid how the pandemic would end, how we would get groceries, and how to protect myself and family. Taking on another stressor did not make sense, but our family chose to do just that and made plans to move to a new house.

Chapter 18
Our New Lives Together

For several years we had talked with our youngest son, Andy, and his wife, Audrey, about the possibility of looking for a house where our two families could live communally. The early years of our oldest son's life were spent growing up with Mel's parents in Escondido and this resulted in his being very connected to his grandparents. However, Andy had only experienced the nomadic life associated with the military and wished he had that connection throughout his youth. After getting married he expressed how important it was to him and Audrey that their children enjoy that sort of relationship with their grandparents. Given the high cost of maintaining two households we began to seriously consider the possibility in the waning months of 2019. We found a house that was the first one all four of us felt would meet our needs and made an offer on a Friday evening. The sellers accepted our offer on Saturday, and this meant we needed to place our house on the market.

On Monday, one of Andy's friends called and said that his family was moving back into the area. This meant his brother and sister-in-law, Josh and Amberlee, who had been renting their home, needed to move. Andy remembered that Josh and Amberlee liked our home, so he called and asked if they were interested in buying it. Since they were looking for a house, they jumped at the chance and both houses were under contract within four days. All of us felt, and still feel, this was a clear answer to our prayers about these matters.

As we moved both of our families into one house, we experienced the normal issues associated with getting organized, deciding where things went and what should be replaced, as well as coordinating each of our expectations and plans for using various rooms. This meant we had to become much better communicators so that we were able to express concerns and come to consensus on everything from the types of window coverings to which pots, pans, and tableware we would use. Although there were additional stressors, I found that recognizing Truman's clues helped me manage my emotional health better. Through all of this transition, Truman and I began to really work together as a team. Soon, everyone in the house began to sense when Truman alerted to my increased anxiety. He was becoming a powerful factor that helped me remain present in discussions as opposed to going to my room, or bed, and avoiding everyone.

For many Americans, the idea of moving into a house with a grown child and their family seems like a lot of headaches. While we have had serious and intense discussions, we understood the reality that in the new COVID world, things were very different. At a time when many grandparents were not able to see their grandchildren, we were with them every day. When the pandemic began Katherine was five and Jennifer two, but they brought a great deal of joy to our lives and helped make the shut-downs bearable. This only added to a sense of peace and comfort when there was tension and sadness just moments before. Like any family, there have been numerous moments when each of us wondered what made us consider something so radical. However, we have remained steadfast with the knowledge that God has been directing all of this.

Shortly after our move, my birth mom fell and was admitted to the hospital. The cause was thought to be a heart issue which could be corrected by implanting a pacemaker. Shortly after having a pacemaker placed in her and being released from the hospital, she fell again. This time she hit her head which caused bleeding in her brain. The prognosis for recovery was not good. Although I felt sad, it was much like my dad's death and my sadness related to the things that could have been as opposed to concern for my mom.

Although my relationship with her remained strained through all of my adult life, I continued seeking opportunities to connect at some level. I had already reestablished a relationship with my sister and youngest brother about eight years prior to my mother's latest injury and I even occasionally entertained the hope that our entire family might find some common ground. However, hopes for any reconciliation were dashed during a trip Shelley and I took to visit my mom several months before her latest injury.

We had planned to take our mom to the doctor and then to lunch. When we arrived, mom verbally assaulted Shelley in a horrific manner. It was as if everything in my sister's life was fair game, and our mom thought vulgarity would enhance her comments. Slut. Whore. Druggie. Loser. These were some of the adjectives being directed at my sister in a rolling onslaught. Just as I was proud of Jim for what he had done to change his life, I was, and remain, proud of Shelley. She left the drug world after three decades, held down a job for over 13 years, and did not blame anyone for what happened in her life. While she had changed for the better, mom had just become angrier at each of her children for not honoring her role as mother and grandmother.

As the tears welled up in Shelley's eyes, it was clear that she was not able to stand up for herself. With no end in sight, I asked my mom to quit talking about Shelley in those terms. I was frustrated and reminded her of all that Shelley had done to improve herself. None of this seemed to matter as our mom was out of control. Instead of changing tones, she turned her attention towards me. I told her that we were done and would leave. Before we left, she wanted us to know that that none of us kids were in her will. This actually made me laugh because I knew her financial situation was anything but solid due to almost $40K in credit card bills and the state of her condo was less than impressive.

When this did not get the desired reaction, she told us she was going to kill herself. If any other person said this, my response would have been much different, but I simply replied, "We will leave and let you do that. Do you want us to call 911 now or just wait a few minutes?" When Shelley and I got to the car, I could no longer hold back my own tears. I was not crying because of the inheritance, or anything said by my mom. Instead, I was ashamed about how callous I had become towards her. My response did not reflect the heart I had sought to foster over the previous forty years. The ease in which those words came out exposed a darker side of my heart. I thought this had been purged, but the contempt and bitterness were still there. When pressure was exerted, my own sinfulness went on display.

It was a difficult trip back to Portland. I was proud of Shelley on so many levels and it only grew when I watched her not retaliate against what my mom said about her. Speaking up for my sister was liberating and helped the contrast between the relationship I had with two of my siblings and our biological mom become much clearer. Before dropping Shelley off at her apartment, I told her that I would not go to see our mom again. I had finally made the break and decided to focus my energy on my relationship with my brother, Mike, and Shelley.

When it came time for my counseling session later that week, I had a whole range of emotions. Most of them were negative and left me drained. My emotional bank was overdrawn, and I became increasingly active and agitated during my nightmares. As such, we began working through them during our sessions. Earlier, in chapter 16, *The Road to Wholeness*, I shared about a question MJ often asked about who else was present during specific events. I saw it as a question related to my family members. However, a few weeks after my trip with Shelley, I was hit with a revelatory thought, "What if MJ is not referring to a person? What if she was asking if I believed the Lord was present when these horrible things happened?"

I was working on one of my counseling assignments when I fully understood that, yes, God was always with me. He had been there through it all. I finally grasped a critical aspect of my faith that moved from my head to my heart. As this realization dawned on me, I could not stop the tears. I thanked the Lord for revealing this truth in such a powerful way. I was almost incapacitated because I was so overwhelmed. This was when the chains I had allowed to hold me down for so long were removed. When I shared this insight with MJ, she recognized that something major had changed in my heart and countenance.

In the following weeks, we continued revisiting the specific nightmare that had plagued me for decades. At what seemed like a glacial pace, things began to change in the nightmare. Truman had done his job each night the terror revisited me and each time I went back to sleep there was additional light radiating in the nightmare. I was finding courage to fight back and not allow my parents or the major to cut me into pieces. Even when my dad was blowing smoke into my mouth and nose, it seemed to be less effective.

On a night after an intense counseling session the most amazing thing happened in my nightmare. My oppressors were pushed aside by an unseen force, and I stood up and began to walk away. I looked back and saw puzzled looks on the faces of my parents and the major. I could faintly hear their voices as they told me they would be nicer but I knew God had delivered me.

Immediately after this I woke up and recalled another powerful dream I had over three decades earlier while stationed at Travis AFB. In it there were telephone poles with lines suspended in the air, only much higher. The wires led to a great light on the horizon, but its radiance was not able to pierce the darkness that surrounded me. I was moving around a grassy area looking at my siblings because they were laying naked and lifeless. I went to each body and tried to revive them but was confused as to why I was ambulatory, but they were dead. I was holding Jim's lifeless form on my lap while crying when a man wearing a hood came and placed his hand on my shoulder. He pointed to the suspended lines, and said, "You must go now, or you will die here too."

As I began climbing the pole, fear gripped me because leaving the area meant I would be leaving everything I knew behind me, something I did not want to do. I kept looking forward at the beaconing light, that seemed too far away to offer any real hope, and my siblings on the ground below. However, the man spoke with a gentle voice to give me the courage I needed to move forward. I began to walk on the narrow lines but turned back when gusts of wind began to blow and caused me to lose my balance. Once back at the pole, I climbed back down, walked over to Jim's still body, and wept. Once again, I was defeated. Once again, I was alone in a dark place. Once again I clung to what I knew because of my fear of the unknown and the lies of the enemy that countered the gentle voice calling me out of the darkness.

I am convinced that both dreams were the result of prayers, and that God was speaking directly to me. The man in the dream was correct, I was dying. Despite not being ready for the truth more than thirty years prior, I finally understood that God had called me to life. I could not fully participate in that life while enslaved by chains.

Since that night, I have never had that nightmare again! It was clear that all of my cries and prayers shouted into the heavens on so many occassions had been answered in a miraculous manner that demonstrated Christ's love and compassion for me. Despite my newly discovered freedom, there were still difficult issues associated with living in a fallen world.

The most difficult issue related to my mom being comatose for months and the reality that someone should be checking in on her. The individual who took this role was Shelley's daughter Dierdra (Dee). Ever since the contentious conversation with my mom, Dee regularly checked in on the wellbeing of my mom. At first, she was puzzled and frustrated because none of my siblings or me wanted anything to do with her grandmother. Each of us had been hurt so many times that we needed distance in order to keep us from becoming overwhelmed by grief, anger, bitterness, and sadness. To her credit, Dee became a vigilant advocate on behalf of our mom.

At one-point the medical staff at the skilled nursing facility informed Dee that our mom's death was imminent. Afterwards, Dee called and told me what was happening. She was beside herself with grief and upset because I did not want to give my mom permission to leave this life and that I loved her. I could not do either of these things with a good conscience. I did not believe my mom needed the former nor did I love this woman on any level. I made it clear that I would not be going up to say anything, nor would I say something over the phone just to assuage someone else. While I hoped her death would be a relief, the process became another burden and pain to bear.

After hanging up, Mel listened to my frustrations and then suggested I might consider reading the letter I had finally written to my mom. I had not considered this while talking with Dee, but it reflected what I honestly felt. While the tone of the three pages reflected great sadness, as opposed to bitterness and anger, the last paragraph was perhaps the best summation of my feelings. I had written, *"… Lately I have dreamed that I am alone, lost, asking for ideas of how to get out of this maze but finding no one to help. There are dead people along the way, but I need to keep going. Then I awaken to tears and sobbing for a long time. There is a great sadness in my heart that I am not able to grieve your leaving us. I feel guilty at times but try to remind myself that God understands both of us. I wish I had confidence that I would see you on the other side because then I would see a different you – one that is really who you were meant to be. It would allow me to weep for joy and hug you in a way that mothers and sons are supposed to do on this side of the veil. My prayer is that even now the Lord might bring a measure of peace into your heart. I think I speak for all of us when I say it is okay to go and that we do not want to see you suffer or linger."*

After rereading this letter, I called my aunt Sharon and read it to her. Like Melody, she too felt it was something that might honor both Dee's request and my convictions so I called Dee and told her Mel and I would be coming up that afternoon.

Despite COVID 19 restrictions on visitors, Dee arranged for both Mel and me to visit my mom so I could read the letter to her. Our drive allowed a couple of hours for Mel and me to talk and pray about what would transpire. What I could not have planned was that the Lion of Judah was on the move again and was about to do another miraculous thing in my heart.

Once we arrived, Dee greeted us and we walked down the hallway to the room where my mom lay. I had no idea what to expect, but I was not prepared for what I saw once we entered her room. Throughout my life, my mom had been extremely obese but there, while transitioning from this life to the next, I saw an unresponsive, slightly overweight, woman with dark circles surrounding her eyes. Instantly, my heart softened. For the first time, I saw her through God's eyes. All the anger and bitterness was replaced with genuine compassion. Without hesitation, I sat by her bedside, gently held her hand, and through tears, read the letter with the most tenderness I have ever had toward her. It was clear that Melody's suggestion was a clear direction from the Lord. Although my mother lingered for several more months, I was finally at peace. Each day the pull of the past experiences became less. In turn, the frequency and intensity of other nightmares were significantly reduced. In turn, this allowed me to consider individuals from my past who had been part of my story. Slowly, I began to consider the possibility that maybe part of my healing involved these people.

Chapter 19
Reconnections

When I left for basic training, I made the decision to distance myself from my family and high school friends. However, the past always impacts our efforts to grow, change, and thrive. Because of this, I was often conflicted about how to interact with a dysfunctional family and being around friends from that time frightened me. I had to weigh the emotional energy expended to connect verses the benefit. This resulted in a part of my life becoming like a black hole because of so much pain from that period of my life. However, as I continued my sessions with MJ in the latter part of 2020, I had a wild thought. I wondered if I could locate some people from that period of my life. This was the first time in over forty years that I considered this but felt it had merit. I began by looking through Facebook and paying a fee to access *Whitepages (Whitepages.com)*, and then made a list of those who impacted my life in a positive way.

My debate partner, Steve Farris, was the first person I looked up. After finding him on Facebook, we began corresponding with each other. In a rather ironic turn of events, I discovered that we both live near Portland, although one city is in Oregon while the other is in Maine. Our interactions also reminded me of the kindness both of his sisters showed me, so I sent them both letters explaining my appreciation. Although I did not hear back from them, it was clear that my interactions with Steve were encouraging and reminded me about some of the better times I had while in high school. The next individual I found was my debate coach, Carol Coe.

I wrote a note and sent it to an address in West Seattle hoping she might actually receive it. Within a couple of weeks, she sent a nice response via email. I was overwhelmed by emotion knowing I could finally thank her for writing the letter that changed the entire direction of my life. Her words swayed the authorities to place me into the foster system as opposed to the juvenile detention program. Although we had written to each other, I wanted to hear her voice and thank her so I called and we talked for quite a while with both of us becoming emotional at various points. Although we would both enjoy seeing each other again, we are waiting until the end of COVID to make this happen. It is not often that one has the opportunity to thank another person for saving your life, but this is exactly what I told her. I was not surprised to learn that after leaving Thomas Jefferson High School she continued teaching, completed her doctorate, and retired as the Washington State Social Studies Superintendent. Looking at my own life, it was clear that the two years spent with her taught me many of the skills that took me through my Master's, writing two books, and working with students who needed someone to see potential in them and become their advocate.

One of the enjoyable things about Facebook is that one can normally scroll through individuals connected to a specific account and discover others you also know. This process allowed me to discover three other people I have been interacting with through email and phone conversations.

Dan Lloyd caught my attention not only because he had remained in the area since we graduated, but also because he has been a pastor for several decades in the city adjacent to where we grew up. He remains a gentleman on every level and pastors a church and also has a rather unique ministry coming alongside people as they grieve the death of a loved one. Both of us enjoy traveling, experiencing other cultures, and are lifelong learners. We have found a kindred spirit in one another on the emotional, physical, and spiritual levels that is more than a little encouraging.

Like Dan, Neal Kuehn is another individual I remembered as being gracious and full of laughter. During one of our conversations a couple months ago there was a bit of a hesitation while I shared about growing up the way I did. He reminded me that we first met in Civil Air Patrol. After telling me this, he shared a difficult part of his own journey. For years he had been angry at his mother because she prevented him from spending time with the major who molested my brother and me. He shared that being able to read the electronic version of this book helped him realize that his mother's actions protected him from being groomed and molested by the major. We were both choked up as he shared this information. His tears came from understanding the protective love of a mother while mine were thankful ones, rejoicing that what I shared helped someone else. When I hung up, I sobbed for quite some time before being able to tell my wife about our conversation.

At the beginning of this book, I shared about neighbors who played a key part in my spiritual life. While the missionaries up the street took us to Vacation Bible School, there was another family who also took us to the same program at their church when the missionaries moved away. The Hallenbeck's were involved in their church and lived two houses down from us. There were three children in the home, but their daughter Deb was closest to my age, and I knew her better than I knew her siblings. As I sought to reconnect with people from high school, I discovered she lives near Bellingham and have been greatly encouraged by her resilience through difficult trials and faith that God is in control. Our conversations about how God has shaped us in the years since K-12 has been a delight. Despite personal heartache, she keeps moving forward and encouraging those around her.

Perhaps the most surprising individual for me to reconnect with has been Marlaine Cover. I did not know her very well in high school and we were in different social circles. However, when looking at the names of friends listed in Steve Farris' profile, I discovered that she authored a book, *Kissing the Mirror*, began a growing non-profit, and has very similar concerns about how we educate students. I reached out to her with little expectation of reconnecting beyond just saying hello. However, while reading her book, I realized that she has really summarized what each of us must do in life; thrive and commune with others. Her own journey has had its share of pain and has given her a compassionate heart. Our interactions have helped me clarify some of my own ideas and encouraged me to continue working towards my own goals. Her enthusiasm and passion for helping others is contagious and the timing of our catching up was nothing short of miraculous as we both were facing difficult issues in our lives and were OK sharing that we did not have it all together and sometimes needed another voice to remind us not only of what we were doing right, but also encouraging one another to have hope.

All of us experience difficult seasons throughout our lives. One of the most troubling seasons for me was while I was a pastor. Although I have forgiven the men who were on the elder board for things that were said and actions taken, I have sought to maintain distance from them. However, towards the end of the summer in 2021, things took a new direction. While shopping at a local grocery store, I noticed one of those men, Dan Rogers. Although I always appreciated his heart for ministry and actually living out his faith, I had little desire to try and connect with him. I have learned that forgiving others does not mean I needed an ongoing relationship with those who hurt me. As such, I greeted Dan kindly and engaged in some small talk expecting to continue with my shopping. However, as I returned to my list, he told me there was something he had needed to share with me for a long time. Although I was content moving along, there was a gentleness and sadness in his tone that brought me back.

Over the next 15 minutes he confessed that he had not been supportive of me while I was the pastor and that he had seen my attempts to really love people. He asked forgiveness for his attitude and his words softened my heart. I told him how much they meant to me and that I had already forgiven him several years before. As we both became teary eyed, a clerk who was restocking the shelves looked down and said, "It's great to see how the body of Christ is supposed to work." As the three of us talked for a few more minutes, I discovered that this young man was praying for us as he listened to our conversation. This encounter was so unexpected and refreshing that I actually forgot to get about half the things on my list but had come home with something much more valuable, a restored friendship.

While it has been important for me to take these steps with people I knew from high school and Dan Rogers, I have also sought deeper connections with my family. Part of this began in earnest shortly after my attempted suicide in 2006 when I wrote a letter to my youngest brother and sister explaining that my life was not what they often thought. I was honest about my gambling addiction during a four-year period, explained how tenuous my emotional balance had been for decades, and shared the truth about our marriage not being as idyllic as they often viewed it.

Those letters allowed them to see me as an equal and that I also had significant flaws. Over the last ten years, this honesty has allowed us to become more open with each other. Both Michael and Shelley have shown great strength as they have overcome every sort of stumbling block that has been placed in their paths. Mike is a master cabinet maker in Indiana and Shelley has been clean and sober for almost two decades and worked full-time job with Wal-Mart for over 14 years. Our conversations have been a source of joy not only for me but for my immediate family as well.

In the months just preceding my mother's death, I made the decision to attend a different church. Although Mel would remain at the church we attended for the previous decade, I believed it was important to see if there was another body where I could use my gifts in a more tangible way and come alongside people who were hurting. Within a few visits, it was clear there was a sense of purpose and direction not only from the leadership, but also within the larger congregation. I was impressed that people were not put off by individuals having tattoos or plugs in their ear lobes. People who have attended church have found this one to be accepting while still holding to what the Bible teaches. As the pastors publicly shared about their own struggles, I noticed that their journeys were similar to my own. Their transparency has allowed me to connect with Christ in a manner I had not experienced before.

Since making the decision to attend Rise, my faith has been challenged in new ways and have taken steps to do things that are way out of my comfort zone. One of the most significant related to a series that talked about the reality that we can never be too far from God. At the end of one of the messages, we were challenged to determine who it was that we had written off and to consider our actions. With little thought, my brother Tony came to mind.

We had not spoken for almost thirty years, but I realized that he is still worthy of dignity. When I arrived home, I began an internet search for him. When I found information that matched his, there were several different addresses. Since I did not know which one was correct, I sent copies of a letter to three different addresses and within a week received an email from him. In it he shared how difficult his life had been, that he had been in the ICU the previous year due to COVID and was frustrated as to why no one ever reached out to him.

My initial reaction was to respond that he could have tried to connect with me as well. However, I knew that was not true because it has taken me years of brokenness, counseling, and serious soul searching before I began to actually thrive and commune well with others. There was nothing I could say to justify my not having reached out sooner. As such, I confessed that it was wrong for me to not have tried to find him sooner. When he asked why I was contacting him when I did, he was surprised when I simply stated, "I was convicted about my attitude when a pastor asked who we had written off." Although his life is complex and difficult, we have begun to talk. I believe the Lord allowed me to hear that sermon so that I would share about God's love, grace, and compassion for Tony through my own actions towards my brother. As my relationships with my siblings has been moving forward, I have also recently been surprised to hear from one of my nieces, Avrial.

She was only five when Jim took his life, but that event has been an extremely heavy burden to her heart ever since. During the week before his death, Jim and his wife had some intense arguments that left Avrial frightened on many levels. On the morning of his suicide, my brother asked Avrial to go to breakfast with him, but she did not want to go. Throughout the last thirty years Avrial believed that if she had gone to breakfast then her dad would not have killed himself. This made his suicide exponentially more difficult to bear. Whereas her mother remarried, little was spoken about Jim after his death and the few years she had with her dad seemed to be almost a dream as the impressions faded. However, late in September of 2021, she reached out to me because she wanted to know more about her dad. This was a plea for help from someone who struggled with many of the same things I have since Jim's death.

During the first week in October, she flew out to Seattle where Avrial, Mel and I stayed in a hotel close to where her dad and I grew up. At first, it was awkward knowing where to begin but we soon began talking about her dad's suicide and life. She wanted to know details about the day he killed himself because she was not really clear about how, or when, things occurred. I was concerned about how she would respond to the details, but she needed to know these things. As I shared, I felt the pain and sadness of Jim's death again but knew Avrial was trying to process it more fully during her visit.

Avrial's mom made the decision to have an open casket at Jim's memorial service. I could not remember whether I was holding Avrial or her sister during the service but recalled that the one I held bent over to kiss Jim. She was immediately confused and terrified because her dad's body was rock hard. I remember holding her closer, trying to comfort her, and asking God why there was so much pain in the world. Avrial shared that she was the one I held and that she remembered being comforted by my actions.

After a few hours of talking, all of us went to bed, but for Avrial and me, it was not the best sleep as we were restless. When we began the next morning, our son in Sandy called and recommended us not bringing Avrial to our home because everyone had COVID like symptoms. So, instead of traveling south, we took a ferry on Puget Sound and relaxed as the previous evening had left us drained. Afterwards, we went by the house where Jim and I were raised followed by a visit to the elementary school we attended. I had not been anywhere near the house for over 30 years and was surprised that much of the strong negative emotions had been replaced with an ability to just speak about the facts of what occurred. While being there was sad, it was the first time it was not overwhelmingly so. However, as we drove to the elementary school, I was overcome by emotion thinking about all the pain we experienced.

When we approached the school, my eyes were drawn to a large black chain that marked an area immediately adjacent to the main entrance. The sword-in-the-stone was always behind those darkened chains, and I wondered if it could still be there? Drawing closer, I discovered that it was exactly where it had been over 40 years before. Without hesitation, I stepped over the chain and touched the artifact. It was as if Jim was there with me, and once again I felt the pain associated with our failed attempts to free ourselves. Both Avrial and I were overwhelmed by our emotions. It was a moment of clarity for both of us. She gained insight into her dad's life, and it was a moment of release for me. For the first time in many years, I longed for Jim and his friendship but was satisfied with the cherished memories we shared. Part of this clarity came from Avrial's sharing about her own memories of her dad. Unfortunately, many of her impressions were very similar to those Jim and I had about our own dad. I tended to gloss over any flaws Jim had because he protected me during those chaotic times at home. However, new information from Avrial allowed me to see that like all of us, Jim was not all good or all evil. This was the first time I really allowed myself to look at him as a whole person. I was also finally able to forgive him for leaving me, for abandoning his kids, and for leaving so many unanswered questions.

When driving Avrial to the airport the next morning, my heart was greatly encouraged because we had finally been able to connect as adults. She was also able to understand more about her dad and some of the difficult things we experienced together. Although the trip was emotional, it was not as overwhelming as I expected and had given me important moments of insight and closure. Even though I have not been able to connect with her sister Jennifer, there is a greater peace knowing that God is in control of the timing for such things.

Chapter 20
Reflections

Writing about my journey has given me the opportunity to look at my life more objectively, put pieces together in a manner I had not considered before, and reflect on important lessons I have learned through all of the experiences. It has reminded me that God not only has been with me through it all but also designed every event to mold, change, and conform me to His own image. I often tease people saying that I would rather take the correspondence course as opposed to going through difficult experiences and yet, these are the very things that have shaped my character and changed my heart. I am sometimes embarrassed because it has taken me so long to not only accept these things but also embrace and be thankful for them. This does not mean I am free of pain in my body or that I no longer battle depression and PTSD. However, having more fully grasped the concept that the Lord really loves me and is always present has comforted me when I feel isolated and anxious. This has helped me to move from despairing of life to finding a greater measure of contentment and peace.

What I once saw as nothing less than torturous, I now see as being transformational. All of it has been part of His process of renewing me. Without serious heartache in my home of origin, brokenness in my mind and body, and literally being able to do nothing but cry out to the Lord, I would not appreciate His grace. All of us go through ordeals that overwhelm us and might even lead us to question His love. However, there is a purpose in all of it. He is always aware of our battles and refuses to give up on those He loves. If I had not gone back through the shattered pieces of my life, this would have remained hidden and trampled by the darkness of everything. Trauma does this. It not only impacted my physical and emotional life, but also affected my spiritual life as well. There have been many occasions when I found it difficult to believe that God is good and yet, none of my experiences have been wasted. In 2 Corinthians 1:3-4 Paul writes, *"Praise be to the God and Father of our Lord Jesus Christ, the Father of compassion and the God of comfort, who comforts us in all our troubles, so that we can comfort those in any trouble with the comfort we ourselves have received from God."* In many ways, coming to the realization that God is sovereign in everything, allowed me to comfort others. The Lord designed the events in my life to mold me in such a manner that I have been allowed to walk with those who are living in that place of desperation where I once lived.

Part of this journey has shown me that God will provide a family, even when our earthly one is dysfunctional. In Matthew 12:48-50, Jesus was interrupted because members of His earthly family were waiting to speak with Him. When hearing this, He asked two rhetorical questions, *"Who is my mother? Who are my brothers?"* He then pointed to the crowd and explained that those who did the will of His Father were His mother, sister, and brother. I spent decades trying to understand what happened to my parents and what caused them to become the people they were. Despite their inability to nurture their children, the Lord has been a real father to me. He has shown great patience, compassion, and love while providing others who became surrogate parents. Like Christ, these men and women have demonstrated unconditional love. They have been there when I have failed and lost hope. They have carried me when I had no strength and did not want to continue living. They have celebrated my victories and rejoiced when I rebounded from the tragedies of loss. They have remained faithful not only to the Lord, but also to me. These are the people who have been my family.

These relationships have not only changed the direction of my life but have been used to help reform my heart. Reflection on many darker times in my life has been difficult because my heart was darkened and the Bible speaks a great deal about the heart, both the darkened and enlightened. I had to face the consequences, or potential for consequences, for foolish things before I accepted that my actions are tied to what was inside one's heart. These moments of insight allowed me to be broken and then built back into something more useful, and powerful, for His Kingdom. This purification has taken place so that I might have compassion for those who are hurting and to come alongside those who find themselves despairing of life.

As you have seen throughout this book, the Lord has used others in this refining process but the main motivation for changing my life has come from spending a great deal of time reading and meditating on the Scriptures. My wife and I are both bibliophiles and constantly have stacks of books near our bedsides. While many authors have helped me gain additional insight into life and encouraged me, it has been through listening to, and reading, the Bible that I have been challenged to look into my heart and make an honest assessment. When I quit seeing the Bible as being just informational and historical, my heart began to change. This has taken a great deal of time and was not easy for me at first. However, like any habit, once I began changing patterns, the results became readily apparent. The Word of God has not only convicted and challenged me, but it has also brought great comfort and joy. It has broadened my understanding of our Risen Lord and allowed me to worship and cry out to Him in ways I had never considered. It has been while reflecting on the Scriptures that I have experienced freedom from the bondage of things that weighed me down and slowed my growth in the spiritual and emotional realms. God has been faithful and did not quit guiding me to important truths and lessons that helped me change my assumptions about life and God.

As I have been writing this final chapter our church has been going through a series entitled, *Wired*. The series has taken one sentence and covered a different aspect each week. This sentence reads:

> ***God created us on purpose, for a purpose and we are empowered for a specific focus, in a particular place, through a unique story, among certain people to live our calling.***

It has been extremely challenging for many because we were encouraged to look at our experiences, relationships, and desires to gain a better understanding of how God has been shaping us. Working through my own story has given me clarity as to how the Lord has been using all of my experiences to prepare me to help a specific group of people; those who experience their own trauma, so that I might encourage them not only through words, but also my own changed heart and life. These changes have profoundly impacted my children and grandchildren as the Lord has changed the trajectory of my life.

One of those miraculous changes has been in our home. Like the area around Puget Sound, there are many damp evenings during the winter here in Sandy and the sky is often heavy with mist, rain, or snow. However, inside our house is the sound of laughter as we sit around the dinner table. While I pray for the meal, Jenny eagerly waits for the end of the prayer to say "Amen!" so she could begin to eat. All of us share about things we have done during the day, the granddaughters tease me, we laugh at their antics, and Audrey shares about movements of the baby she carries inside and will deliver in July. It is a place of peace, joy, and love. Later, we read books to the girls, play games together, and find restful sleep on most nights.

I cannot say why the Lord has done this for me while I see others struggling with life. However, I am convinced that it has been a work of grace and that I am not to squander the opportunities the Lord gives me. He has worked mightily so that I might come alongside others. He calls me not to affluence and a life of ease, but to a life of sharing and serving. He changed me not so I can boast about my abilities or hoard things for myself but so that I might minister to and with others to offer the hope only He can give. The Lord's work in rescuing my heart and life has not only changed the direction of two more generations within our family but is also changing the direction of many who I have been able to come alongside and walk through the various seasons of life together. It has been through each of life's experiences that I have come to know the character of my God. It is what has allowed me to experience joy and given me real hope. As such, I give Him praise, and worship Him as my Lord. It allows me to bow down and be still in His presence knowing He is merciful and compassionate.

Today, when I look towards the heavens and cry out to God, my tears flow because of the lavishness of His love and grace that the Lord has shown me. For all of it, I give thanks to the Risen Lord.

About the Author:

John Mayner and his wife, Melody, live communally with their youngest son and his family in Sandy, OR, retired from the Air Force after 27 years of service, and holds an M.Div from Multnomah Biblical Seminary. He enjoys ocean fishing, scuba diving, and almost any seafood. Other pastimes include playing board games, smoking meats, and discussing movies and current events. He is available for speaking engagements at churches as well as conferences and retreats.

He can be reached at: myopenfaithjourney@gmail.com

About the Editor:

Stephanie Anderson is a natural light photographer and freelance editor based in Troutdale, Oregon. She has worked as an editor for author Randy Alcorn, including on his books *Does God Want Us to Be Happy?*, *Face to Face with Jesus*, and *Giving Is the Good Life*. You can find her online at www.stephanieellice.com.